"*Heirs of the Covenant* is a great resource for the life of the Church. In this classic work, Susan Hunt demonstrates how an understanding of God's covenant informs and empowers our ministry of discipleship. Using practical examples, she presents how the covenant works out in the life of individuals, families, local churches, and the community. The goal of covenantal discipleship is to lead God's people to think and act with hearts set on Christ, through whom we enjoy all of the benefits of being children of God."

**Dr. Stephen Estock**
Coordinator, Committee on Discipleship Ministries
Presbyterian Church in America

"I began using this book in children's ministry courses but quickly realized from the reaction of students that the material was a great primer for covenantal theology. Not only is the material presented in a theologically consistent manner, but also included are very practical applications of covenantal theology for the Christian education program of the local church. I use the material from the book in teacher training workshops and Sunday school classes, as well as on the seminary level. This book helps people understand quickly, and clearly, the importance of covenantal theology."

**Dr. Barksdale Pullen**
Pastor of Community Life
Wildwood Church, Tallahassee, Florida

"*Heirs of the Covenant* beautifully explores God's plan for his people to teach their children within both the home and the church. Susan Hunt passionately calls everyone in the church to delight in our covenant privileges and responsibilities to raise the next generation of kingdom disciples. No other resource combines such rich theology with a practical framework for true, covenantal discipleship. By His grace may we hold before our children the love and faithfulness of our covenant-keeping God and teach them to trust and obey King Jesus so that they may arise and boldly labor to leave a legacy of faith to the next generation."

**Jeremy Case**
Children's Ministry Director
Perimeter Church, Johns Creek, G

D1270276

*A Biblical Legacy of Faith for All Generations*

# Heirs

## *of the*

# Covenant

SUSAN HUNT

**GREAT COMMISSION**
PUBLICATIONS

This edition published in 2014 by Great Commission Publications.

Great Commission Publications
3640 Windsor Park Drive
Suwanee, Georgia 30024
www.gcp.org

Previously published in 1998 by Crossway Books, a division of Good News
Publishers, 1300 Crescent Street, Wheaton, Illinois 60187.

Cover design: Chris Tobias

Printed in the United States of America

ISBN 978-0-9833580-5-3

# CONTENTS

*Acknowledgments*     9

*Foreword*     11

*Introduction*     13

1   The Content of the Covenant     *17*

2   The Context of the Covenant     *43*

3   The Book of the Covenant     *65*

4   Home and Church     *87*

5   A Covenantal Strategy for Church Growth     *111*

6   Teaching Covenantally     *135*

7   A Strategy for Christian Education     *159*

8   The Villagers and the Village Life     *185*

9   For Christ's Crown and Covenant     *211*

*Notes*     *235*

# DEDICATION

My husband, Gene, teaches me the content of the covenant in the context of covenant love. This book is as much his as it is mine. Together we dedicate it to:

Our son and sons-in-love,

Richie Hunt
Dean Barriault
Scott Coley

With praise to God for His grace in them and with gratitude to them for teaching our grandchildren the content of the covenant in the context of covenant love.

*Know therefore that the Lord your God is God;*
*he is the faithful God, keeping his covenant of love*
*to a thousand generations of those who love*
*him and keep his commands.*
*—Deuteronomy 7:9*

# ACKNOWLEDGMENTS

It is quite disconcerting to have your name on the cover of a book that you feel you did not write. First of all, this book is from God and unto Him. Second, He sent numerous covenant-keepers who surrounded me with their knowledge, skills, encouragement, and love. Their names should be on the cover of this book. I can only mention a few, but my deep appreciation goes to them all.

Dennis Bennett, Sharon Betters, Lynn Brookside, Allen Curry, Charles Dunahoo, George and Karen Grant, Sue Jakes, Tom and Jane Patete, Paul and Georgia Settle, and Barbara Thompson read the chapters, shared their wisdom, and allowed me to get credit for their ideas.

The Tuesdays Together Women's Bible Study and The Racerunners Sunday school class of Midway Presbyterian Church deserve gold medals for patience. They listened to me ramble until my thoughts clarified, they asked questions that made me think more precisely, they cheered me on, they enfolded me in love, and they prayed for me.

The men and women who wrote the stories at the beginning of each chapter and the men and women they wrote about give vitality to this book. I am blessed by them, and I believe you will be.

Gene, our children, our grandchildren, and my mother daily show me the splendor of God's covenant faithfulness to families. They are what this book is about . . . they are "my joy and crown" (Philippians 4:1).

# FOREWORD

Cornelius Van Til wrote, "We have found in the covenant and in the creation idea a divine ordinance for education. Our educational program as involved in the covenant idea is based upon the concept of creation, and the concept of creation is once more based upon our idea of God. And as for our idea of God, we hold to it not as a moral or mental luxury but as the very foundation of the structure of human experience."[1] This statement underscores the importance of this book.

Much of the individualistic framework of our Western world does not see training, educating, and equipping in its broader community setting. This is even true with the Christian community. True, substantive education is Christian education. It teaches the truth about God from His Word. God gives this process to parents and churches; hence it is covenant education. Susan Hunt understands this and has successfully taught it for many years.

*Heirs of the Covenant* is not a diagnostic book of present challenges, opportunities, and problems in education. It is a book that sets forth the right premises and seeks to develop them in a workable manner for both home and church. In an easily readable manner, Susan takes the teaching part of the Christian community's assignment to "make disciples" and places it in a framework that is thoroughly biblical.

*Heirs of the Covenant* will help families and the Christian community work together in the context of God's covenant promises. Since our purpose is to know God and to know His Word, we need God-centered resources and methods to help us communicate our faith to our children and our children's children. The inroads of modernism and postmodernism into our culture present a huge challenge to families and churches. This book will be a tremendous resource to better equip us to reach a crucially important generation.

*Heirs of the Covenant* will enhance church growth while developing ways to renew or revitalize a church. Covenant education helps us remember who we are, why we are here, and the legacy we must pass on to the present and future generations. God has given us so much, and we are responsible to bequeath that gift to our children. How we communicate God's truth and teach His Word must be built upon a strong biblical and theological base if our teaching and discipling are to have any lasting results. Susan Hunt demonstrates a remarkable understanding of our biblical heritage and trust, and she knows how to communicate those truths in a practical way. As a father, teacher, and professional educator, I highly commend *Heirs of the Covenant*.

—Dr. Charles H. Dunahoo
Coordinator, Christian Education and Publications
Presbyterian Church in America

# INTRODUCTION

Six months after I finished college, I felt led to go into vocational ministry. It was 1962. If the controversy about ordaining women to the pulpit ministry was brewing, I was totally unaware of it. I did what young women in my denomination did who wanted to pursue vocational ministry; I attended seminary and began work on a degree in Christian education with the goal of being a DCE (Director of Christian Education). This was a viable and accepted ministry track for women.

I got the degree and a job in a church in our seminary community. Even more exciting, I married a seminary student. When Gene graduated, we were off to our first church. We both had a heart for Christian education, and over the years we had wonderful hands-on experiences in developing programs and in refining our theology and philosophy of Christian education in the home and in the church. But somewhere along the way, Christian education in the church at large seemed to take a nosedive. Gene and I were so busy raising a family and serving our congregations that we did not notice. It was almost as if one day we looked around and realized to our dismay that Christian education had diminished in importance. Few Christian colleges or seminaries offered CE degrees, and few churches employed anyone in this position.

I am sure there are many reasons for this. The rise of some movements within the church contributed to the demise of others. But I wonder if one reason Christian education lost its influence is that the controversy over ordaining women was no longer brewing; it was stewing. This made everyone, including me, gun-shy. In our reaction to this trend, we threw the proverbial baby out with the bath water. We overreacted and retreated to a position that left no church staff ministry options for women. Because we objected to the ordination of women, we feared allowing women into any ministry positions.

I am sad that women are not encouraged to pursue this ministry venue, because it seems to me that women are well suited to the nurturing, detailed, creative work of Christian education in the local church. But I am most sad that for whatever reason, Christian education has lost its appeal in the modern church. I think the reason is much deeper than "a gender thing."

As I reflect on this phenomenon, I realize that my conclusions are more intuitive than investigative. Deep inside I have a strong conviction that Christian education's tailspin was due to a diminishing emphasis on theology. Various scholars have chronicled the history and the effect of this shift (*No Place for Truth* by David Wells is an excellent example). But the question that plagues me is, if theological leakage was the downfall of Christian education, who de-emphasized theology? Wouldn't it be those of us who were involved in Christian education? Could it be that to some extent we bought into flashy evangelical fads and trends rather than resolutely teaching God's people to think theologically? Most of us did not reject the importance of theology; we just became trendy. We assumed that everyone was in theological agreement, and our students drifted into theological ignorance. Then our programs became structure without substance, and soon there was no need for the structure.

I will not spend pages cataloging the consequences. One example is sufficient. According to George Barna's research, the only significant difference between Christians and non-Christians is that Christians go to church more often, give more money to the church, and own more Bibles. Other indicators, such as the number who believe the Bible is absolute truth, the divorce rate, and alcoholism are essentially the same.

My prayer is that we will recapture our passion for the substance. The structure will take shape if the substance is there.

Those of us who are passionate about teaching God's people to think and live Christianly must stop whining about the lack of attention given to Christian education. We must step up to the plate and assume our responsibility. Moms and dads, grandparents, Christian day school teachers, Sunday school teachers, youth leaders, and pastors must do the grunt-work of teaching God's people line upon line, precept upon precept. We must stop going for the gold and go for the mind and heart. Some say we have probably lost this generation of young people. I am not willing to give up without a fight. But the only thing substantive enough to claim and reclaim this generation is the Gospel of grace "because it is the power of God for the salvation of everyone who believes . . ." (Romans 1:16).

The Gospel of grace is the message of the sovereign King of the universe entering into a relationship with His people. How could such a thing happen? It took a covenant.

Much has been written about the *content* of the covenant, but little about the day by day, week by week, generation by generation privileges and responsibilities of living in covenant with God and with His people. This book will consider how the *content* of the covenant is lived out in the *context* of the covenant community, and how it *culminates* in authentic Christianity.

This book is about Christian education, not only in the narrow sense of programs and classrooms, but in the covenantal sense of the people of God living in covenant with Him and with one another.

Christian education must be *intentionally covenantal,* or it will simply be a feeble attempt to sanctify the world's philosophies and methods by scattering some Bible verses through them.

Christian education must be *integratively covenantal,* or it will degenerate into insipid moralism that aims for behavioral change apart from grace.

Christian education must be *inclusively covenantal,* or it will fragment the people of God into artificial age divisions that rob them of learning from and growing with one another.

This book has a limited scope. It will explore the whys and hows of being intentionally, integratively, and inclusively covenantal as we live out our relationship with Jesus Christ.

Though this book is written for the individual reader, greater benefit will come when groups of people study it together. It can be used by Sunday school classes and Bible studies, in intergenerational studies with teens and adults, by groups of parents and their teens, and for teacher training in the educational ministry of the home, church, and Christian day school. A Leader's Guide with complete lesson plans for interactive studies is available. Call 1-800-283-1357.

A final disclaimer. I am surprised that I am writing this book. I have believed for years that it should be written but thought someone else should write it. I am neither a theologian nor a scholar. But God would not excuse me for those reasons. In fact, I finally concluded that because this book is not *for* theologians and scholars, God would use an ordinary person to write it so that ordinary people would use it. This is Christian Education 101.

May God give us Christian education crusaders who are committed to leaving a legacy of faith for the next generation.

*Glorify the Lord with me;*
*let us exalt his name together.*
—*Psalm 34:3*

# 1

## The Content
## of the Covenant

Our son Richie is a husband, father, full-time college student, and part-time Director of Children's Ministry in our church. He is praying about what the Lord wants him to do after graduation. He wonders if the Lord is calling him to full-time children's ministry.

One day as we talked about this, I asked some questions: "Why do you believe a church should have a strong children's ministry? When you recruit teachers, why do you think they should be involved in this ministry? What would drive you to do this full-time?"

Without hesitation he said, "I want the kids to know and love Jesus, and I want them to have such strong relationships with people in the church that they will not drift away during their teen years."

My response: "That's commendable, and the programs you have put in place are an affirmation of your vision and your passion. But your vision and your passion will never empower you to go the distance. You will fizzle along the way. I think your vision and passion have theological roots, but you must know that in your own mind and heart. Whether you do this as a vocation or as a volunteer, you must be able to clearly articulate a theological reason for what you do. You must have a biblical apologetic for an educational ministry."

His question: "What do I need to know?"

This is what I told him. . . .

---
∾
---

LIVING AND TEACHING
COVENANTALLY

## THE LEGACY

A line of Christian educators left a rich legacy in Scotland.

Young Patrick Hamilton of Scotland was a gifted student. In pursuit of his studies, he traveled to the university of Wittenberg where he met Martin Luther and Philip Melancthon, leaders in the new Reformation movement.

> By these distinguished masters he was instructed in the knowledge of the true religion, which he had little opportunity to become acquainted with in his own country, because the small remains of it in Scotland at this time were under the yoke of oppression. . . . He made an amazing proficiency . . . and became soon as zealous in the profession of the true faith, as he had been diligent to attain the knowledge of it. . . . He came to the resolution of returning to his own country, and there, in the face of all dangers, of communicating the light which he had received. Accordingly, being as yet a youth, not being much past twenty-three years of age, he began sowing the seed of God's word wherever he came. . . .[1]

Hamilton became a master of the object lesson technique of teaching. He was the object. The authority of God's Word was the lesson. In 1527, at age twenty-four, he was burned at the stake. He was the first martyr in Scotland for the cause of the Reformation, but he was not the last. As the fire blazed around him, he cried out, "How long, O Lord, shall darkness overwhelm this realm? How long wilt Thou suffer this tyranny of men? Lord Jesus, receive my spirit."[2]

Following Hamilton's death, many Protestant leaders took

refuge abroad. In 1544, when the persecution of Protestants was raging, George Wishart returned to his homeland and resumed his preaching and teaching. Two years later he too was burned at the stake. When Wishart was arrested, one of his students insisted on remaining with him. Wishart sent him away with the words, "Return . . . and God bless you. One is sufficient for a sacrifice." That student was John Knox who became, in the words inscribed on a monument to his memory in Glasgow, "the chief instrument, under God, of the Reformation of Scotland."

Knox, a champion of Christian education, said, "Seeing that God has determined that His Church here on earth shall be taught not by angels but by men, it is necessary to be most careful for the virtuous education and godly upbringing of the youth of this realm." His leadership in establishing schools to instruct young people and his fiery, uncompromising preaching prepared a people to live uncompromisingly through political and ecclesiastical turmoil. His teaching also prepared his family to be steadfast.

Knox's daughter Elizabeth married John Welch, a minister who was known for his faithful preaching and fervent prayer life. He would rise from his bed all during the night and pray. One night Elizabeth heard him pray, "Lord, wilt Thou not grant me Scotland?" and after a pause, "Enough, Lord, enough." Later, when she asked what he meant by "Enough," he told her that he had been

> wrestling with the Lord for Scotland and found there was a sad time at hand, but that the Lord would be gracious to a remnant. . . . He continued the course of his ministry in Ayr till King James's purpose of destroying the Church of Scotland by establishing bishops was ripe, and then it became his duty to edify the Church by his sufferings, as formerly he had done by his doctrine.[3]

He was arrested in 1605. Elizabeth tirelessly sought her husband's release. When she finally received an audience with King James, she was announced as Knox's daughter and Welch's wife.

The king finally said that if she could persuade her husband to submit to the bishops, he would be released, but Elizabeth refused to compromise. She lifted her apron and resolutely replied, "I'd rather have his head in this." Her husband remained in prison.

In February 1638, the National Covenant was drafted, and copies were carried all over Scotland. Thousands signed this document that rejected the Divine Right of Kings in favor of man's duty to God. Lord Warriston, one of the drafters of the document, called it "The great Marriage Day of this Nation with God."[4] The persecution of the covenanters became so intense that the 1680s are known as the Killing Time. History brims with stories of the uncompromising heroism of these men and women.

There was Captain John Paton, who in his dying testimony at the place of execution said:

> I bless the Lord I am not come here as a thief or murderer, and I am free of the blood of all men, and hate bloodshed. . .and now I am a poor sinner, and never could merit anything but wrath; and I have no righteousness of my own; all is Jesus Christ's, and His alone. . . . The Council asked me if I acknowledged authority. I said, all authority according to the word of God. . . . Now I leave my testimony as a dying man against that horrid usurpation of our Lord's prerogative and crown-right; I mean that supremacy established by law in these lands, which is a manifest usurpation of His crown, for He is given by the Father to be Head of the Church. . . . Farewell, sweet Scriptures, preaching, praying, reading, singing, and all duties. Welcome, Father, Son, and Holy Spirit! I desire to commit my soul to thee in well-doing! Lord, receive my spirit![5]

And the minister John Brown, whose wife and children watched as he was shot in the head. Before the trigger was pulled, he said, "Well, now, Isabel, the day has come that I told you would come when I first spoke of marrying you."

She replied, "Indeed, John, I can willingly part with you."

His response: "Well, that's all I desire. I have nothing more to do than to die. I have been in this happy estate to meet with death for many years." He kissed the children and prayed that God's blessings would fall upon them.

The merciless captain of the dragoons pulled the trigger and then turned to Isabel and said, "What do you think of your fine husband now?"

Her steady response: "I ever thought much good of him and more than ever now."

What drove these people? Why did they go to such extremes? What could possibly have evoked such radical obedience?

The banner of the covenanters says it all. Their rallying cry was "For Christ's Crown and Covenant." The King of Glory entered into a covenant of grace to save His people. His crown rights over them and His covenant of love to redeem them are worthy of uncompromising allegiance.

# The Content
# of the Covenant

~

At the dawn of human history, God said, "Let there be light."
And there was light.

His sovereign authority was established. He made it. It is His.
He is the King.

The rest of creation followed in the same fashion. God spoke.
It happened. Then He created man and woman.

> *Then God said, "Let us make man in our image, in our like-*
> *ness, and let them rule over the fish of the sea and the birds of*
> *the air, over the livestock, over all the earth, and over all the*
> *creatures that move along the ground." So God created man*
> *in his own image, in the image of God he created him; male*
> *and female he created them. God blessed them and said to*
> *them, "Be fruitful and increase in number; fill the earth and*
> *subdue it. Rule over the fish of the sea and the birds of the air*
> *and over every living creature that moves on the ground."*
> —*Genesis 1:26-28*

The account of the creation of man teems with a heightened
familial tenderness, thrill, and purpose.

## PLACE AND PRESENCE

Gene and I recently built a new home. After years of living in a church
manse, it was exhilarating to plan and prepare a place specifically for
our family. We designed a house with lots of "gathering space" for our
children and grandchildren. It was thrilling to watch the architect's

plans become a foundation, then a frame, and finally a house. But the thrill fades when compared to snuggling with a grandchild between us and hearing that child say, "I love you." The house is a place for us to enjoy each other. It is a place for us to be together. It is a place for Gene and me to gather our children and grandchildren around us and to say in many different ways, "I love you." But it is the presence of our family that makes the place wonderful.

Creation was the house. Adam and Eve were the children. God did not prepare the place and leave. He visited the place He prepared for Adam and Eve. He talked with them. The place was magnificently beautiful, but the splendor of it was God's presence. His presence gave it purpose. His presence made it safe. His presence filled it with joy and love. His presence gave it life.

It was not man's presence that made the place glorious. It was God's presence. Some say God made man because He was lonely and needed someone to love. That is preposterous. God is complete in Himself. There is perfect fellowship within the Trinity. It is His presence that completes us.

## THE COVENANT OF WORKS

When God created Adam, He made a covenant with him. A covenant is a binding agreement with specific terms. The promise was God's presence. This is amazing because the Creator entered into an arrangement in which the creature had a claim. The Creator obligated Himself to the creature. The condition was perfect obedience. God would keep the covenant promise. Adam must obey the covenant obligation. He could not eat the fruit of the tree of the knowledge of good and evil. This was the test. This would demonstrate Adam's conscious acceptance of the covenant promise. This is called the covenant of works, but it does not mean that Adam worked to earn his relationship with God. God sovereignly initiated that relationship. It means that Adam had to make a choice to remain in God's presence by subjecting himself to God's authority.

While Adam and Eve lived in God's presence, they reflected

His glory to one another and to creation. So they lived in harmony with one another and with creation.

But Adam ate the forbidden fruit. He broke covenant. His covenant-breaking severed his perfect relationship with God. Because God is holy, there can be nothing unholy in His presence. His holiness will consume anything unholy. Now when Adam and Eve faced each other, and when they faced creation, they reflected their own selfishness. Adam was our representative in the covenant agreement. The consequences of His covenant-breaking thundered through creation, through history, and into every human heart.

## THE COVENANT OF GRACE

One night after hearing the story of Adam and Eve, our three-year-old grandson Mac prayed, "Dear God, please let Adam and Eve go back to the Garden."

The good news is that God did just that. It was not a return to the literal Garden, but He made a way for them to return to His presence.

God was not obligated to do anything. He could have turned away from the creature and the creation. Instead He intervened. He came to the Garden. He called to the man. And He clothed Adam and Eve in garments of skin (Genesis 3:8, 9, 21). Here is the essence of the covenant of grace—God came, He called, He clothed. God comes to us while we are dead in our trespasses and sins (Ephesians 2:1-9). He calls us into a relationship with Himself (Acts 2:38-39). And He covers our guilt with the perfect righteousness of Christ so that we can once again live in His presence (Isaiah 61:10)—glorious, sovereign grace from beginning to end.

It has to be that way. The penalty of sin is death. And dead people can do nothing—absolutely nothing—to regain life.

As *The Westminster Confession of Faith* says:

The distance between God and the creature is so great, that although reasonable creatures do owe obedience unto Him as their Creator, yet they could never have any fruition of Him as their blessedness and reward, but by some voluntary condescension on God's part, which He hath been pleased to express by way of covenant.[6]

In *The Christ of the Covenants*, O. Palmer Robertson writes:

Some would discourage any effort to present a single definition of "covenant" which would embrace all the varied usages of the term in Scripture. They would suggest that the many different contexts in which the word appears imply many different meanings. Clearly any definition of the term "covenant" must allow for as broad a latitude as the data of Scripture demands. Yet the very wholeness of the biblical history in being determined by God's covenants suggests an overarching oneness in the concept of the covenant. What then is a covenant? How do you define the covenantal relation of God to his people? A covenant is a bond in blood sovereignly administered. When God enters into a covenantal relationship with men, he sovereignly institutes a life-and-death bond.[7]

When God came to the Garden, He made a promise to the man, and He pronounced a curse upon Satan. "I will put enmity between you and the woman, and between your offspring and hers; he will crush your head, and you will strike his heel" (Genesis 3:15).

In his landmark work, *Promise and Deliverance*, S. G. DeGraaf said, "In principle, the whole of redemption is revealed in the mother-promise (Genesis 3:15)."[8]

This was not the establishment of the covenant of grace; it was the revelation of that covenant. This covenant was not established with Adam, but with Christ. This covenant was not an afterthought. It was not made in response to man's sin. The divine agreement to redeem man was in place before man was created. Jesus, the Mediator and Head of this covenant, is the "Lamb that was slain from the creation of the world" (Revelation 13:8).

Because redemption was in the divine will of God, it was the same as done. "He will crush your head" was not a hoped-for future event; it was an accomplished fact. Neither were the beneficiaries of the covenant an afterthought. "For he chose us in him before the creation of the world to be holy and blameless in his sight. In love he predestined us to be adopted as his sons through Jesus Christ, in accordance with his pleasure and will—to the praise of his glorious grace, which he has freely given us in the One he loves" (Ephesians 1:4-6).

In the first glimpse of this "mother-promise," God reveals Jesus the Mediator who will crush the head of Satan and win the victory over sin and death. Even while Adam and Eve are trying to hide their nakedness, God tells them about Jesus.

In spite of man's performance, God returned to the Garden and said, "I will still be your God; you will be My people; I will provide the way for you to live in My presence; I will dwell among you." This is grace. It is undeserved. Adam demonstrated his belief in the promise by naming his wife Eve, which means life. He believed that she would bear children, including the Child who would leave the glory of God's presence in order to secure a place for us in God's presence.

Throughout the rest of Scripture, God unwraps His covenant promise that He is our God, that we are His people, and that we live in His presence. Perhaps you have received a gift wrapped in a large box. You open it to find a smaller box, and then with growing anticipation you open another and another, until finally you come to a tiny box with the precious gift. Read these verses as though you are opening that gift, until finally you reach the tiny box (a manger) with the precious Gift (the Christ Child).

God said to Abraham:

> *I will establish my covenant as an everlasting covenant between me and you and your descendants after you for the generations to come, to be your God and the God of your descendants after you.*
>
> *—Genesis 17:7*

*I will take you as my own people, and I will be your God. Then
you will know that I am the LORD your God, who brought
you out from under the yoke of the Egyptians.*

—Exodus 6:7

*You are standing here in order to enter into a covenant with
the LORD your God, a covenant the LORD is making with
you this day and sealing with an oath, to confirm you this
day as his people, that he may be your God as he promised
you and as he swore to your fathers, Abraham, Isaac and
Jacob.*

—Deuteronomy 29:12-13

*When all the work Solomon had done for the temple of the
LORD was finished . . . the temple of the LORD was filled with
a cloud, and the priests could not perform their service
because of the cloud, for the glory of the LORD filled the temple of God. Then Solomon said, ". . . I have built a magnificent temple for you, a place for you to dwell forever."*

—2 Chronicles 5:1, 13-14; 6:1-2

*I will give them a heart to know me, that I am the LORD. They
will be my people, and I will be their God, for they will return
to me with all their heart.*

—Jeremiah 24:7

*I will bring them back to live in Jerusalem; they will be my
people, and I will be faithful and righteous to them as their
God.*

—Zechariah 8:8

Then it happened. God came to live among us in the flesh.

*The Word became flesh and made his dwelling among us. We
have seen his glory, the glory of the One and Only. . . .*

—John 1:14

Even His name confirms the promise.

*The virgin will be with child and will give birth to a son, and they will call him Immanuel—which means, God with us.*
*—Matthew 1:23*

While He was among us, He told us about the place where we will live in His presence for eternity.

*In my Father's house are many rooms. . . . I am going there to prepare a place for you. And if I go and prepare a place for you, I will come back and take you to be with me that you also may be where I am.*
*—John 14:2-3*

But until we go to that place, He gave us a task and the promise of His presence as we obey His command.

*Go and make disciples of all nations, baptizing them in the name of the Father and of the Son and of the Holy Spirit, and teaching them to obey everything I have commanded you. And surely I am with you always, to the very end of the age.*
*—Matthew 28:19-20*

To keep that promise, He sent His Spirit to live in us, and the dwelling place changed from a hill to a heart.

*Do you know that your body is a temple of the Holy Spirit? . . . For we are the temple of the living God. As God has said: "I will live with them and walk among them, and I will be their God, and they will be my people."*
*—1 Corinthians 6:19; 2 Corinthians 6:16*

There is more to come. The ultimate fulfillment will be realized in the new Jerusalem.

*Then I saw a new heaven and a new earth, for the first heaven and the first earth had passed away, and there was no longer any sea. I saw the Holy City, the new Jerusalem, coming down out of heaven from God, prepared as a bride beautifully dressed for her husband. And I heard a loud voice from the throne saying, "Now the dwelling of God is with men, and he will live with them. They will be his people, and God himself will be with them and be their God. He will wipe every tear from their eyes. There will be no more death or mourning or crying or pain, for the old order of things has passed away." He who was seated on the throne said, "I am making everything new!" Then he said, "Write this down, for these words are trustworthy and true."*

—*Revelation 21:1-5*

The revelation of the covenant in the Old Testament is progressive. The series of covenant relationships with Noah, Abraham, Moses, and David do not replace each other. They supplement each other. And the revelation of this divinely instituted relationship reaches its climactic fulfillment in the new covenant when the Seed of the woman crushes the head of the serpent.

## CHARACTERISTICS OF THE COVENANT

Entire books are written about the covenant, so obviously this is not an exhaustive statement of its characteristics. I do not in any way intend to minimize the rich complexity of this doctrine. These are simply a few of the characteristics that are pertinent to the purposes of this book and that will be developed throughout the remainder of the book.

The covenant is *relational because it is restorative.* "In its most essential aspect, a covenant is that which binds people together. Nothing lies closer to the heart of the biblical concept of the covenant than the imagery of a bond inviolable."[9] The covenant reconciles us to God and defines the way we live in relationship with Him. He refers to us in tender, relational language as His children (Deuteronomy 14:1), His treasured possession (Exodus 19:5). We are given specific promises, obligations, responsibilities, and privileges. The covenant also establishes and defines our relationships with one another as God's children. When Jesus was asked which is the greatest commandment, He answered in relational language: "'Love the Lord your God with all your heart and with all your soul and with all your mind.' This is the first and greatest commandment. And the second is like it: 'Love your neighbor as yourself'" (Matthew 22:37-39).

2.    The covenant is *sovereignly initiated.* Jesus said, "You did not choose me, but I chose you and appointed you to go and bear fruit—fruit that will last" (John 15:16).

3.    The covenant is *sovereignly sustained* and thus *eternally secure.* God is a covenant-keeper who is able to keep us in the palm of His hand. "My sheep listen to my voice; I know them, and they follow me. I give them eternal life, and they shall never perish; no one can snatch them out of my hand. My Father, who has given them to me, is greater than all; no one can snatch them out of my Father's hand. I and the Father are one" (John 10:27-30).

4.    The covenant is *Trinitarian*. God the Father made a covenant with His Son. If Jesus would pay the penalty for sin and be the substitute, God would give Him a people. The Holy Spirit was also a party in this covenant. He would be the one who would regenerate God's people. He would give them a new heart so they could believe. This is the covenant of grace. The Father purposed redemption. Jesus accomplished redemption. The Holy Spirit seals it to our hearts (Ephesians 1:3-14).

5.    The covenant is *corporate.* The first Adam represented all mankind. The second Adam, Christ, represented His people before the judgment seat of God. As DeGraaf wrote, "In the covenant God always draws near to His people as a whole—never just to individuals. Because of the covenant, the entire people rests secure in God's faithfulness, and every individual member of the covenant shares in that rest as a member of the community."[10]

Each individual must respond in faith, but the covenant is not individualistic, because Christ is the Mediator on behalf of His people. The Lord said to Abraham, "I will make you into a great *nation* . . ." (Genesis 12:2). The angel said to Joseph, ". . . you are to give him the name Jesus, because he will save *his people* from their sins" (Matthew 1:21). Paul wrote to the church in Ephesus, "You were separate from Christ, excluded from citizenship in Israel and foreigners to the covenants of the promise, without hope and without God in the world. But now in Christ Jesus you who once were far away have been brought near through the blood of Christ. Consequently, you are no longer foreigners and aliens, *but fellow citizens with God's people and members of God's household"* (Ephesians 2:12-13, 19).

The covenant is *generational*. God's faithfulness is generational: "The children of your servants will live in your presence; their descendants will be established before you" (Psalm 102:28). Our responsibility is generational. The promises, privileges, and obligations are to be passed from generation to generation. "I will utter hidden things, things from of old—what we have heard and known, what our fathers have told us. We will not hide them from their children; we will tell the next generation the praiseworthy deeds of the LORD, his power, and the wonders he has done. He decreed statutes for Jacob and established the law in Israel, which he commanded our forefathers to teach their children, so the next generation would know them, even the children yet to be born, and they in turn would tell their children" (Psalm 78:2-6). Peter accentuated this generational characteristic in his sermon at Pentecost when he said, "The promise is for you and your children and for all who are far off—for all whom the Lord our God will call" (Acts 2:39).

The covenant is *compassionate*. When Moses asked to see God's glory, God put him in a cleft in the rock, covered him with His hand, and passed in front of him proclaiming, "The LORD, the LORD, the compassionate and gracious God, slow to anger, abounding in love and faithfulness" (Exodus 34:6). God's people show His glory through ministries of compassion done in His name. Jesus said that when we help the hungry, thirsty, sick, the stranger, and the prisoner, we do it for Him; when we fail to help them, we do not show His glory (Matthew 25:31-46).

(8)     The covenant is *integrative*. It is the underlying unity of Scripture. It is the framework through which we look at Scripture. Thus it should integrate, order, and govern our thinking about the world and about our lives. It centers all of life on Jesus. A comprehensive, unifying world and life view begins with God. He is our reference point. In Him we "live and move and have our being" (Acts 17:28). Our purpose is to glorify Him. This is why "The fear of the LORD is the beginning of wisdom" (Psalm 111:10). It is why we should pray, "Teach me your way, O LORD, and I will walk in your truth; give me an undivided heart, that I may fear your name" (Psalm 86:11). So the covenant should regulate the education of God's people.

(9)     The covenant is *exclusive*. "You shall have no other gods before me. You shall not make for yourself an idol. . . . You shall not bow down to them or worship them; for I, the LORD your God, am a jealous God. . ." (Exodus 20:3-5). We cannot serve two masters (Matthew 6:24).

(10)     The covenant is *inclusive*. In the Old Testament, God worked primarily in and through the nation of Israel. In the New Testament, the doors fling open to include Jew and Gentile. We are commissioned to "Go into all the world and preach the good news to all creation" (Mark 16:15). And John wrote that he saw a Lamb, encircled by the four living creatures and twenty-four elders, who sang: "You are worthy to take the scroll and to open its seals, because you were slain, and with your blood you purchased men for God from every tribe and language and people and nation" (Revelation 5:9).

## WHAT IS MY COVENANT PRIVILEGE?

Jesus won for me the thrilling privilege of living in the presence of God. Moment by moment, day by day, year in and year out, God's people live in His presence.

An understanding of God's covenant promise to be our God,

and a realization that this does not depend on our performance but on His provision, ushers us into the glorious truth that we live in His presence. His presence gives us purpose. His presence makes us safe. His presence fills us with joy and love. His presence is our life.

Moses understood this, and he would settle for nothing less. In Exodus 3 we read that he was in the desert, tending the flock of his father-in-law, when "the angel of the LORD appeared to him in flames of fire from within a bush. . . . God called to him from within the bush. . . . God said, 'Take off your sandals, for the place where you are standing is holy ground. . . . I am the God of your father, the God of Abraham, the God of Isaac and the God of Jacob'" (Exodus 3:2-6).

Moses was in the desert. He was at work. But he was on holy ground because God was there. Living in the presence of God means that we are always on holy ground. His presence makes all of life sacred. For the Christian, there is no division between sacred and secular. All of life is sacred because it is lived for His glory and in His presence. All of life is to be brought under His lordship.

After leading the Israelites out of Egypt and after receiving the Ten Commandments, Moses came down from Mount Sinai and found the people worshiping the golden calf. God told Moses to leave and take the people to the land He had promised. Then God said, "but . . ." and it is what follows this conjunction that makes the critical difference. "But I will not go with you, because you are a stiff-necked people and I might destroy you on the way. When the people heard these distressing words, they began to mourn . . ." (Exodus 33:3-4).

For God to withdraw His presence was reason for distress and mourning. Moses went before God, not because the people deserved it, but because of God's covenant promise.

*Moses said to the LORD, "You have been telling me, 'Lead these people,' but you have not let me know whom you will send with me. You have said, 'I know you by name and you*

*have found favor with me.' If you are pleased with me, teach
me your ways so I may know you and continue to find favor
with you. Remember that this nation is your people."*

*—Exodus 33:12-13*

Moses knew that the line of demarcation was the presence or
absence of God. The place would be empty without God's presence. And the only hope for God's presence was that He had
promised that He would be their God and they would be His people. The only hope was the covenant. Moses' confidence was His
knowledge that God is a covenant-keeper.

*The LORD replied, "My Presence will go with you, and I
will give you rest." Then Moses said to him, "If your
Presence does not go with us, do not send us up from here.
How will anyone know that you are pleased with me and
with your people unless you go with us? What else will distinguish me and your people from all the other people on the
face of the earth?"*

*—Exodus 33:14-16*

In the remainder of this incredible encounter, Moses asks to see
God's glory. God put Moses in a cleft in the rock and covered him
with His hand. Then God passed by.

*Then the LORD came down in the cloud and stood there with
him and proclaimed his name, the LORD. And he passed in
front of Moses, proclaiming, "The LORD, the LORD, the compassionate and gracious God, slow to anger, abounding in
love and faithfulness, maintaining love to thousands, and forgiving wickedness, rebellion and sin. Yet he does not leave the
guilty unpunished; he punishes the children and their children for the sin of the fathers to the third and fourth
generation."*

*Moses bowed to the ground at once and worshiped. "O
LORD, if I have found favor in your eyes," he said, "then let*

*the LORD go with us. Although this is a stiff-necked people, forgive our wickedness and our sin, and take us as your inheritance."*

*Then the LORD said: "I am making a covenant with you. Before all your people I will do wonders never before done in any nation in all the world. The people you live among will see how awesome is the work that I, the LORD, will do for you. Obey what I command you today."*

—*Exodus 34:5-11*

Then God gave covenant responsibilities. The people were to rid the land of false worship and false worshipers. They were not to coexist with unbelief. Moses was on the mountain forty days. And God wrote on the tablets of stone the words of the Ten Commandments.

The conclusion of this drama is riveting:

*When Moses came down from Mount Sinai with the two tablets of the Testimony in his hands, he was not aware that his face was radiant because he had spoken with the LORD.*

—*Exodus 34:29*

The privilege of living in the presence of God results in a radiance of life that cannot be denied. Living in His presence empowers us to reflect the glory of the Glorious One. What an awesome privilege.

### WHAT IS MY COVENANT RESPONSIBILITY?

Covenant-keeping is evidence of our covenant relationship with God. Covenant-keeping is necessary to enjoy covenant blessings. Obedience does not earn entrance into God's presence. Obedience validates the reality of that relationship. "If you love me, you will obey what I command" (John 14:15).

God has sovereignly drawn us into a relationship with

Himself. We have the glorious privilege of living in His presence. Enjoying this privilege requires an intentional, disciplined pursuit.

It means we must "demolish arguments and every pretension that sets itself up against the knowledge of God, and we take captive every thought to make it obedient to Christ" (2 Corinthians 10:5).

It means we are not to "conform any longer to the pattern of this world, but be transformed by the renewing of your mind . . ." (Romans 12:2).

It means that whether you "eat or drink or whatever you do, do it all for the glory of God" (1 Corinthians 10:31).

Living in His presence will distinguish us from all the other people on the face of the earth (Exodus 33:16). When we live in His presence, we see His character. Then we turn and face every human relationship and situation and radiate His character.

A COVENANT-KEEPER

Mrs. Johnston lived in God's presence and radiated His character. She was one of the most powerful teachers I ever had, though I never saw her stand before a class. She was in her seventies when I met her. She joined our church, and many of us were never the same. She quietly taught us by her cheerful spirit, her gentle words of encouragement, and her constant love for God and His Word.

When Mrs. Johnston was confined to a bed in a nursing home, I often took my Sunday school class of first through third grade children to visit her. They would sing, recite memory verses, and listen as she told them about our wonderful Savior. Then they would form a line and take turns giving her a hug. Even as she grew increasingly frail, she delighted in the children, and they knew it.

One day, as the last child left her room, she took my hand and said with fervency, "They will not forget that you brought them." And she was right. She was thanking me and saying it was a good thing for a Sunday school teacher to do, but the reason they did not forget is because of what she taught them, not because of what I did.

One Sunday after she died, our lesson was about joy. I began the lesson by asking, "Can anyone tell me what joy is?"

Without a moment's hesitation a child said, "Mrs. Johnston." No one snickered. The children knew the right answer had been given.

Mrs. Johnston taught those children, and me, what it means to live in God's presence. The place did not matter. Her bed in a nursing home was holy ground because God was there. She celebrated His presence and radiated His character.

She was a true Christian educator.

Postscript: When the children and I squeezed into the elevator after our visits with Mrs. Johnston, I would always say, "One day you will be Sunday school teachers, and what will you do?"

They responded, "We will take the children to visit older people."

I would then ask, "Whom will you visit?"

Their response: "You!"

Think about it.

TAKE-AWAY POINT

> *I press on to take hold of that for which Christ Jesus took hold of me. Brothers, I do not consider myself yet to have taken hold of it. But one thing I do: Forgetting what is behind and straining toward what is ahead, I press on toward the goal to win the prize for which God has called me heavenward in Christ Jesus.*
>
> *—Philippians 3:12-14*

God's presence is the prize. His character is our hope to win the prize. His sovereignty means He is *able* to keep every covenant promise. His faithfulness means He *will* keep every promise. His sovereign faithfulness describes His eternal love.

His Crown and Covenant are our hope, our joy, and our goal.

∾

*Question:* What is the covenant of grace?

*Answer:* It is the King of Glory's binding promise that He will be our God, that we will be His people, and that He will live among us. It is the sovereignly initiated arrangement by which He keeps that promise.

## BECOMING A COVENANT-KEEPER

1. Do you have a relationship with God through faith in Jesus Christ? If not, I urge you to acknowledge your sinfulness and your need of a Savior. Cast yourself on His mercy, ask His forgiveness, and embrace Jesus as your Savior.

2. Read Ephesians 1. Write out what each member of the Trinity did and does for your salvation. Rejoice over the work of the triune God on your behalf.

3. Read Exodus 33 and 34. Does God's presence distinguish you from all others on the face of the earth? Do you radiate His glory? List the covenant responsibilities in this passage. Ask God to show you any "foreign gods" in your life and to give you grace to demolish them.

4. Is there a "Mrs. Johnston" in your life? Thank him/her for radiating God's presence to you.

5. Are you a "Mrs. Johnston" to those around you? Pray about it.

## CHRISTIAN EDUCATION IDEA

Use the verses listed below for a Bible drill. This can be done with adults or children, or with teams of combined ages at intergenerational gatherings such as family devotions or a church family night supper. In the first set of verses, each verse refers to God as our

King. In the second set, each verse contains the covenant promise: I will be your God; you will be my people; I will live among you. After the first set is read, ask what we learn about God in these verses. Following the second set, ask what promise is repeated in every verse. If no one knows, repeat the drill until someone gets the answer. Give that person or team extra points.

These verses refer to God as King:

Psalm 24:7-10
Psalm 44:4
Psalm 47:6-7
√ Psalm 145:1
Isaiah 6:5
Isaiah 44:6
Zephaniah 3:15
John 12:13
1 Timothy 1:17
Revelation 17:14

These verses contain the covenant promise:

Genesis 17:7
Exodus 6:7
Leviticus 11:45
Leviticus 26:12
Deuteronomy 7:6
Deuteronomy 29:12-13
Jeremiah 24:7
Jeremiah 31:33
Zechariah 8:8
2 Corinthians 6:16
Titus 2:14
Hebrews 8:10
Revelation 21:3

Following the drill, explain that this is God's covenant promise to His people. Ask questions such as:

1. What do you think about when you think of a king?

2. What does it mean to you that the King of Glory has promised to be our God and to accept us as His children?

3  What does it mean to you that God has promised to live among us and that we live in His presence? What difference does this make in your work and your play, in your choices and priorities?

4. What does it mean to you that God has promised never to leave you?

You may want to make a banner with a cross and crown and the words, "For Christ's Crown and Covenant."

# 2

*The Context
of the Covenant*

---

∾

---

## LIVING AND TEACHING
## COVENANTALLY

### TWO TEACHERS

Joni Eareckson Tada and Howard G. Hendricks are two of today's outstanding Christian educators.

From her wheelchair, Joni Tada has taught God's truths through her books, art, music, and radio program. Through the organization Joni and Friends, she has equipped and mobilized churches to minister to people who have disabilities.

Dr. Hendricks, professor of Christian Education at Dallas Theological Seminary, author, and speaker, has cast a vision for Christian education and equipped and motivated God's people to teach His Word.

Their ministries have influenced multitudes, and both of them acknowledge the influence of a teacher in his/her own life.

Joni remembers a Young Life worker in the high school she attended. "Marcia and her roommate would invite us high school girls to drop by their apartment on Tuesday mornings before school for a snack. She made even orange juice and doughnuts seem so special. The table was set with fresh flowers, brightly colored cloth napkins, and the nicest china. I was impressed that she cared so much about something so incidental! After our time of talking and snacking, she would read something from the Bible. We would all pray briefly and then go on our way to school. Those short moments one morning a week paved the way for me to enter the kingdom of Christ. Marcia, in her quiet, consistent way, dropped the seeds of God's Gospel in my heart and gently watered and nurtured my life in Christ into full bloom. I thank her for that."[1]

Dr. Hendricks tells about Walt, a tall, caring man who couldn't wait until a Sunday school class was available for him to teach. He went out and found his own class by making friends with thirteen boys. He played marbles with them and got to know them. Dr. Hendricks says, "I didn't care where he wanted me to go; I wanted to follow him! He was our friend as well as our teacher. He listened to my problems by the hour and even helped me with my homework. Then one Sunday he made the Gospel so clear that I gave in. That day Christ became my Savior, and He changed my life. In fact, eleven out of the thirteen boys Walt recruited from our neighborhood eventually entered vocational Christian work!"[2]

Marcia and Walt—two Christian educators whose ministries have been multiplied through the students they loved and taught.

# The Context
## of the Covenant

∾

Scripture clearly teaches that the content of God's covenant is to be contextualized in the covenant community. If the covenant is taught in a purely academic way, it will be anemic. God never intended the passing on of the covenant to be just a mental exercise. The covenant is corporate. Our relationship with God is personal and individual, but when that relationship is established, we are immediately in community with others who are in relationship with Him. His grace-relationship with us is the *power* that transfers us from the City of Destruction into the Community of Faith and the *pattern* for how we are to relate to others in this community.

There is a correlation between the *content* of the covenant and the *context* of the covenant relationship of God's people with one another. The content of the covenant is to be pushed out into all of life.

Be assured that this is not a relational model built on sentimentalism and felt-needs theology. It is a relational model built on the covenant of grace. There is a huge difference. The reference point for a needs-based model is experience and feelings. The reference point for a covenant model is God and His Word. The first exalts self. The second exalts God.

## COGNITIVE AND EXPERIENTIAL

The content and the context of the covenant are woven together in Scripture, and they must be delicately woven together in the education of God's people. So this education is both cognitive and experiential. It is formal and informal. It is head and heart. It must get into the mind and the muscles.

Moses understood this content-context synthesis. He told the Israelites to teach the covenant promises and commands to their children "when you sit at home and when you walk along the road, when you lie down and when you get up" (Deuteronomy 6:7). But Moses knew that it would take more than this informal, experiential approach. It would also take intense formal instruction. God's covenant had to be the reference point for their life experiences, or the experiences would become the reference point. So just before Moses' death he "wrote down this law and gave it to the priests. . . . Then Moses commanded them: '. . . Assemble the people—men, women, and children, and the aliens living in your towns—so they can listen and learn to fear the Lord your God and follow carefully all the words of this law. Their children, who do not know this law, must hear it and learn to fear the Lord your God as long as you live in the land you are crossing the Jordan to possess'" (Deuteronomy 31:9-13).

The concept of a covenant community is so foreign to our fallen natures that our redeemed natures struggle to believe and practice it. The cultural bent to privatization and individualism is nothing new. It is simply a group picture of the bent of our sin nature. It started in the Garden when Adam blamed Eve and refused to accept responsibility for their actions. It was dramatically perpetuated in their son Cain. After Cain murdered his brother, God asked, "Where is your brother Abel?" Cain's response is the response of fallen man: "I don't know. Am I my brother's keeper?" (Genesis 4:9). Cain was clueless that the answer is *yes*. We are our brother's and sister's keepers.

It is interesting that though community goes against the grain of our fallen nature, we want to be part of a group. We like to run in packs. We like to have a buddy. We want to feel accepted by a group. This need has intensified today, and the church is capitalizing on it with a major emphasis on small groups, care groups, affinity groups, support groups, and any other kind of group that can be imagined.

These attempts to meet felt needs are too often form without substance. They are based on a sinful need to "make me feel better" rather than on a holy desire to reflect my covenant relationship with the Lord God by loving my brothers and sisters the way our Father loves me. The church should be zealous to cultivate community among believers. But unless the members of the community understand that the covenant community was established by an act of God's free grace and that their existence and purpose is about His glory and not their personal happiness, they will lack the substance to sustain the structures they put in place. If the groups are self-determined and self-focused, they will fizzle out when each individual's needs are not met.

## ADOPTION—
### ENTRY TO THE COVENANT COMMUNITY

God's adoption plan was put in place before time began. "For he chose us in him before the creation of the world to be holy and blameless in his sight. In love he predestined us to be adopted as his sons through Jesus Christ, in accordance with his pleasure and will . . ." (Ephesians 1:4-5).

When God adopts us into His family, we become joint heirs with His only begotten Son, Jesus, and with His other adopted children. We are family. God adopts us into His family on the basis of the finished work of Jesus Christ on our behalf. There is nothing about us that caused Him to choose us to bear His name. Community life in the church will be just as vain and vacuous as life in any other community unless it is grounded on our adoption.

In answer to the question, "What is adoption?" *The Westminster Shorter Catechism* responds: "Adoption is an act of God's free grace, whereby we are received into the number, and have a right to all the privileges of the sons of God."[3]

*The Westminster Confession of Faith* states:

> All those that are justified, God vouchsafeth, in and for His only Son Jesus Christ, to make partakers of the grace of adoption, by

which they are taken into the number, and enjoy the liberties and privileges of the children of God, have His name put upon them, receive the spirit of adoption, have access to the throne of grace with boldness, are enabled to cry, Abba, Father, are pitied, protected, provided for, and chastened by Him, as a Father: yet never cast off, but sealed to the day of redemption; and inherit the promises, as heirs of everlasting salvation.[4]

Paige Benton is on staff with Reformed University Ministries at Vanderbilt University. In one of her newsletters she wrote in characteristic fashion:

> ... Today is Christmas Eve. So *of course* we had to put up the tree tonight. And we do win the tacky ornament trophy— from plastic wise men to Smurfs (we just can't accept that they're New Age).
>
> Let me interrupt myself—this is a newsletter. ... I've spent many hours this semester with a junior who is a baby Christian. After several meetings her gregarious excitement about the Lord calmed down just enough for me to sense an unspoken, gnawing uncertainty in her. Convinced of the genuineness of her conversion, I again explained that justification is a legal verdict in the court of heaven that no force of sin or fading love on our part can change. Still uncertain. I encouraged the use of the means of grace. She dived in—uncertainty lingered. We looked at passages teaching God's preservation of His people. She underlined them but still no confidence.
>
> What had I left out? ADOPTION! This girl was living like a foster child, at the heart of which is the whole concept of *probation*. When I told her that she is actually a daughter of God in Christ, that the Father loves her as much as He loves His own Son, that she could not be forsaken unless Jesus is cast out of heaven ... well, let me just say that she's a different kid, and our times together are not searches but celebrations.
>
> Now, back to tree decorating tonight. Why does my mama (who has considerable class, by the way) insist on hanging

these redneck relics? Simple. Because they're ours—Louis's, Laura's, mine. She doesn't see aluminum, felt, plastic, shrink-art. She sees us at ages three, eight, eleven, fourteen. Just like always, she decorates the tree for her children.

You want to know something amazing? The Lord Jesus is decorated *with* His children! Why does almighty God insist on clinging to us fallen, useless relics? Simple, because we're His. The Father doesn't see our pitiful tackiness; we look just like His Son to Him. Wrapped up in Christ, we are jewels, lights, treasure, stars, the very twinkle in His eye. I can't wait to be back and tell my young friend that we are not just the King's daughters; we are His *ornaments!*

Just think, my whole job is to tell students that we are the Heir's inheritance, the keepsakes of His grace. Are you jealous, or what?[5]

The covenant community is not a self-centered attempt to meet my needs. The covenant community is a wild and wonderful conglomeration of God's children, most of whom probably have very little in common except our kinship with our Elder Brother Jesus. But it is this kinship that binds us together in an eternal bond. God establishes this community. It is our privilege and responsibility to maintain, nurture, and cultivate a community life that will be a compelling evidence of our adoption.

When we realize that our adoption is permanent, we have the courage to celebrate our identity by looking and acting like our Father. We recognize and love our brothers and sisters because they look and act like Him too. But even when they fail to have a family resemblance, we love them because our Father loves us when we fail to resemble Him.

## OLD TESTAMENT LESSONS

From the beginning God dealt with families. Then He took one of those families and promised, "I will make you into a great nation"

(Genesis 12:2). Old Testament Israel is a physical picture of the spiritual reality of the church. The Old Testament stories and celebrations teach us about the covenant way of life.

One of those celebrations was the sign of the covenant which was given to believers and their children. God told Abraham, ". . . You must keep my covenant, you and your descendants after you for the generations to come. . . . Every male among you shall be circumcised. . . . It will be the sign of the covenant between me and you. For the generations to come every male among you who is eight days old must be circumcised. . . . My covenant in your flesh is to be an everlasting covenant. Any uncircumcised male, who has not been circumcised in the flesh, will be cut off from his people; he has broken my covenant" (Genesis 17:9-14). This mark of identification is a sign to point us to the promise that "I am your God, you are My people, I live among you," and it is a seal that this promise has the authority of the King. It was also a sign of community solidarity. Anyone who was not circumcised was cut off from his people. Since the resurrection of Jesus, the sign and seal of our relationship with Christ is baptism.

Another celebration was the Passover. When the moment arrived in Israel's history for their deliverance from bondage in Egypt, God did not speed up the process. He planned it so that the people lingered over every detail of the event in such a deliberate manner that they would reenact it for generations to come. Each family went through the exact ritual at the exact time as every other family in the covenant community. God said to Moses:

*Tell the whole community of Israel that on the tenth day of this month each man is to take a lamb for his family. . . . Take care of them until the fourteenth day of the month, when all the people of the community of Israel must slaughter them at twilight. Then they are to take some of the blood and put it on the sides and tops of the doorframes of the houses where they eat the lambs. . . . The blood will be a sign for you on the houses where you are; and when I see the blood, I will pass over you. . . . This*

*is a day you are to commemorate; for the generations to come*
*you shall celebrate it as a festival to the LORD. . . . And when*
*your children ask you, "What does this ceremony mean to*
*you?" then tell them, "It is the Passover sacrifice to the LORD,*
*who passed over the houses of the Israelites in Egypt and*
*spared our homes when he struck down the Egyptians."*
                                        —Exodus 12:3-27

The simultaneous reenactment of this celebration by each family
surely contributed to community solidarity. Since the resurrection
of Jesus, our Passover Lamb, this sign and seal of God's covenant
promise is the Lord's Supper.

During the wilderness wanderings, even the arrangement of
the family dwellings was a reminder of the promise, "I am your
God, you are My people, I live among you." God gave Moses
explicit instructions for building the tabernacle. Everything about
this structure is a picture of the gospel message. Moses carried out
every detail of the construction as the Lord commanded him.
"Then the cloud covered the Tent of Meeting, and the glory of the
LORD filled the tabernacle. . . . So the cloud of the LORD was over
the tabernacle by day, and fire was in the cloud by night, in the sight
of all the house of Israel during all their travels" (Exodus 40).

The Lord told Moses to put the tabernacle in the middle of the
camp. "The Israelites are to camp around the Tent of Meeting some
distance from it, each man under his standard with the banners of
his family. . . . So the Israelites did everything the LORD commanded Moses; that is the way they encamped under their standards, and that is the way they set out, each with his clan and
family" (Numbers 2).

No matter where you lived, when you stepped out of your tent,
you saw glory. The centrality of God's presence dominated community life.

When Israel was settled in the land of the promise, the temple
replaced the tabernacle. Solomon built the temple on the very site
where centuries earlier Abraham was poised to sacrifice his son

Isaac but received instead a substitute—a lamb caught in a thicket. At the dedication service, Solomon prayed, and then "fire came down from heaven and consumed the burnt offering and the sacrifices, and the glory of the LORD filled the temple" (2 Chronicles 7:1). After almost a month of celebrating, the people returned to their homes, and God and Solomon had a talk.

> *The LORD appeared to him at night and said: "I have heard your prayer and have chosen this place for myself as a temple for sacrifices. When I shut up the heavens so that there is no rain, or command locusts to devour the land or send a plague among my people, if my people, who are called by my name, will humble themselves and pray and seek my face and turn from their wicked ways, then will I hear from heaven and will forgive their sin and will heal their land. Now my eyes will be open and my ears attentive to the prayers offered in this place. I have chosen and consecrated this temple so that my Name may be there forever. My eyes and my heart will always be there."*
> *—2 Chronicles 7:12-16*

What a promise! The glorious reality is that now we don't have to step outside our tents to be reminded of God's presence. We only have to look inside our hearts. "Do you not know that your body is a temple of the Holy Spirit, who is in you, whom you have received from God?" (1 Corinthians 6:19). The temple is no longer on a hill. It is in the hearts of God's people.

The promise is the same: "I have chosen and consecrated this temple so that my Name may be there forever. My eyes and my heart will always be there."

Because of the covenant, the King's eyes and heart are always on His church . . . *if* . . . if God's people live together in humility, if we pray and seek His face and turn from our wicked ways, then the glory of His presence will rest upon us and will distinguish us from all the other people on the face of the earth (Exodus 33:16).

God's eyes and heart are on us individually, but when we

gather as His church, that glory should be such a dazzling spectacle of grace that the very culture we live in will be touched by that grace.

God then told Solomon, "Do all I command, and observe my decrees and laws" (2 Chronicles 7:17). These are educational issues. God's people must be taught the decrees and laws. They must be taught how to live covenantally before Him and with one another.

## NEW TESTAMENT LESSONS

The New Testament is the fulfillment of the promise given in the Old Testament. Jesus is the message of both testaments. He is the Mediator of the covenant. He is our Kinsman-Redeemer who pays the redemption price to purchase us for His Father. He is our Elder Brother who shares His inheritance with us. The New Testament is about our personal redemption, but it is also about our corporate identity.

Jesus made it absolutely clear that the identifying mark of this community is love. "A new commandment I give you; Love one another. As I have loved you, so you must love one another. By this all men will know that you are my disciples, if you love one another" (John 13:34-35).

Following Peter's Pentecost sermon, the people "were cut to the heart and said . . . 'Brothers, what shall we do?' Peter replied, 'Repent and be baptized, every one of you, in the name of Jesus Christ for the forgiveness of your sins. And you will receive the gift of the Holy Spirit. The promise is for you and your children and for all who are far off—for all whom the Lord our God will call. . . .' Those who accepted his message were baptized, and about three thousand were added to their number that day" (Acts 2:37-39, 41).

And immediately community life began.

*They devoted themselves to the apostles' teaching and to the fellowship, to the breaking of bread and to prayer. Everyone was filled with awe, and many wonders and miraculous signs were done by the apostles. All the believers were together and had everything in common. Selling their possessions and*

*goods, they gave to anyone as he had need. Every day they*
*continued to meet together in the temple courts. They broke*
*bread in their homes and ate together with glad and sincere*
*hearts, praising God and enjoying the favor of all the people.*
                                                    —*Acts 2:42-47a*

There was teaching and fellowship—content and context—
and the result was dramatic. "And the LORD added to their number daily those who were being saved" (Acts 2:47b).

Paul wrote to the church in Ephesus: ". . .You are no longer foreigners and aliens, but fellow citizens with God's people and members of God's household, built on the foundation of the apostles
and prophets, with Christ Jesus himself as the chief cornerstone. In
him the whole building is joined together and rises to become a
holy temple in the LORD. And in him you too are being built
together to become a dwelling in which God lives by his Spirit"
(Ephesians 2:19-22).

Peter wrote to the church scattered throughout Pontus, Galatia,
Cappadocia, Asia, and Bithynia, "But you are a chosen people, a
royal priesthood, a holy nation, a people belonging to God, that you
may declare the praises of him who called you out of darkness into
his wonderful light. Once you were not a people, but now you are
the people of God; once you had not received mercy, but now you
have received mercy" (1 Peter 2:9-10).

Citizenship in the community is not optional for God's children. We are part of the family. However, some treasure this citizenship, while others are ignorant of it or indifferent about it. The
value we place on our citizenship privileges and responsibilities is
a strong indicator of the quality of our relationship with the King
of this kingdom.

HISTORICAL EXAMPLE

The Puritans probably give us the clearest example since the New
Testament of the content of the covenant formulating a concept of

community. In 1630 eleven vessels arrived on the shores of Massachusetts. John Winthrop, the leader of the group, wrote a lay sermon entitled "A Model of Charity" in which he "expressed his intention to unite his people behind a single purpose—the creation of a due form of government, ecclesiastical as well as civil, so that their community would be a model for the Christian world to emulate. Theirs was to be, he said, a 'City upon a Hill.'"[6] After giving the reasons for and characteristics of such a community, he concluded with these fervent words:

> Now the only way to accomplish this end and to provide for our posterity is to follow the counsel of Micah, "to do justly, to love mercy, and to walk humbly with our God." For this end we must be knit together in this work as one man; we must entertain each other in brotherly affection; . . . we must delight in each other, make other's conditions our own, rejoice together, mourn together, labor, and suffer together, always having before our eyes our commission and community in this work, our community as members of the same body. So shall we keep the unity of the Spirit in the bond of peace. The Lord will be our God and delight to dwell among us, as His own people, and will command a blessing upon us in all our ways, so that we shall see much more of his wisdom, power, goodness, and truth than formerly we have been acquainted with. We shall find that the God of Israel is among us—when ten of us shall be able to resist a thousand of our enemies, when He shall make us a praise and glory, that men shall say of succeeding plantations: The Lord make it like that of New England. For we must consider that we shall be as a City upon a Hill. . . .
>
> "Beloved, there is now set before us life and good, death and evil, in that we are commanded this day to love the Lord our God, and to love one another to walk in His ways and to keep His commandments and His ordinance, and His laws, and the articles of our covenant with Him that we may live and be multiplied, and that the Lord our God may bless us in

the land whither we go to possess it. But if our hearts shall turn away so that we will not obey, but shall be seduced and worship other gods, our pleasures, and profits, and serve them; it is propounded unto us this day, we shall surely perish out of the good land whither we pass over this vast sea to possess it."

Therefore let us choose life that we, and our seed may live; by obeying His voice, and cleaving to Him, for He is our life, and our prosperity.[7]

This concept was shaped by the Puritans' strong theology. Their systematic Christocentric approach to faith and life was clearly documented in *The Westminster Confession of Faith*. The chapter on "Of the Communion of the Saints" states:

All saints, that are united to Jesus Christ their Head, by His Spirit, and by faith, have fellowship with Him in His grace, sufferings, death, resurrection, and glory: and, being united to one another in love, they have communion in each other's gifts and graces, and are obliged to the performance of such duties, public and private, as do conduce to their mutual good, both in the inward and outward man.

Saints by profession are bound to maintain an holy fellowship and communion in the worship of God, and in performing such other spiritual services as tend to their mutual edification; as also in relieving each other in outward things, according to their several abilities and necessities. Which communion, as God offereth opportunity, is to be extended unto all those who, in every place, call upon the name of the Lord Jesus.[8]

All who are united to Jesus are united to one another in love. We are *obliged* to share our gifts and graces with one another. We are *bound* to maintain a holy fellowship. These are strong words to the self-centered, felt-needs orientation of today's churchgoer. The church must not capitulate to this orientation. We must counteract it by teaching the content of the covenant in the context of an authentic covenant community that values our covenant privileges and responsibilities.

## HINDRANCES

Many things make it difficult to follow the covenant way of life today, but there have always been barriers to living covenantally. Our own sinful desires join forces with the alien culture to wage an ongoing battle for our allegiance. Then there are the realities of our modern age. Many of us live in areas where our lives do not intersect except at church. We don't see fellow church members at the supermarket or at work or at the soccer field. Combine this with age-segregated specialized ministries at church, and community life is marginalized.

These hindrances do not excuse us. They simply mean that we must intentionally face them head on and enthusiastically cultivate community life in our churches. But we must never put community structures in place without carefully teaching *why* we do *what* we do. Christ's Crown and Covenant must be the impetus, the vision, and the treasure of our covenantal community life.

## FAMILY TREASURE

After a magnificent doxology of praise to the supremacy of Christ, Paul wrote to the church in Colosse: "My purpose is that they may be encouraged in heart and united in love, so that they may have the full riches of complete understanding, in order that they may know the mystery of God, namely, Christ, in whom are hidden all the treasures of wisdom and knowledge" (Colossians 2:2-3). This is a clear statement of the necessity of head and heart involvement in church life.

The treasure is Christ Himself. Knowing Him unlocks precious treasures of wisdom and knowledge. But notice that Paul wants the Colossians to cultivate an environment of encouragement and unity that reflects the reality of Christ *so that* they may discover these treasures.

The treasures will be understood at a deeper level when our hearts are encouraged and we are united in love. When there are family squabbles or even insensitive indifference, we forfeit some of our inheritance.

Learning to share our gifts and graces with one another so that members of the church family are encouraged in heart and united in love is an educational process. Just as we have to teach our children how to treat one another, our Father God teaches us in His Word that we are to serve one another (John 13:1-15), to "be devoted to one another" (Romans 12:10), to "be kind and compassionate to one another, forgiving each other" (Ephesians 4:32), to "encourage one another" (Hebrews 3:13), and to "pray for each other" (James 5:16).

But God does not just give us a list of house rules. He gives us grace to follow the rules. His Spirit produces the fruit of love, joy, peace, patience, kindness, goodness, faithfulness, gentleness and self-control (Galatians 5:22-23) that enables us to act like our Father. And our Elder Brother intercedes for us before the Father's throne.

## OUR ELDER BROTHER'S PRAYER

Just before His arrest, trial, and crucifixion, Jesus prayed. In this prayer, He embraces all believers for all ages. He prayed for you and for me.

> *My prayer is not for them alone. I pray also for those who will believe in me through their message, that all of them may be one, Father, just as you are in me and I am in you. May they also be in us so that the world may believe that you have sent me. I have given them the glory that you gave me, that they may be one as we are one: I in them and you in me. May they be brought to complete unity to let the world know that you sent me and have loved them even as you have loved me.*
> —John 17:20-23

The world will believe that God sent Jesus because they will not be able to deny the evidence in His children. Selfish individualism is our natural inclination. When the world sees true unity/community, they have to reckon with the reality of something they cannot imitate. But this unity is impossible apart from the glory of God's presence, which is His gift to us.

In this prayer, we see Jesus' heart. "Father, I want those you have given me to be with me where I am, and to see my glory, the glory you have given me because you loved me before the creation of the world" (John 17:24).

Amazing! The only begotten Son longs to share His rightful inheritance with His Father's adopted children. And He wants us to have some of the inheritance right now. "Righteous Father, though the world does not know you, I know you, and they know that you have sent me. I have made you known to them, and will continue to make you known in order that the love you have for me may be in them and that I myself may be in them" (John 17:25-26).

Jesus continues to make the Father known to us through His Word and Spirit. The more we know the Father, the more we will reflect Him to each other. The more we are filled with His love, the more we will love each other. This is what will distinguish our community from all other communities on the face of the earth.

To know the content of the covenant of grace and to fail to touch our brothers and sisters with that grace is a denial of the power of that grace. However, the loving unity of the covenant community is compelling evidence to the world of the reality of the Gospel.

### TAKE-AWAY POINT

I used to laugh when my mother showed me a family relic and said, "Now remember, this is not junk. It is the butter mold your great-grandmother used. When I've gone to heaven, don't sell this in a yard sale."

I don't laugh anymore. I have even videotaped her telling the stories of these cherished keepsakes. I want to be sure I get the stories right when I tell them to our grandchildren.

Gene and I are becoming increasingly deliberate and intentional in planning for family vacations and celebrations that create memories and that perpetuate traditions. We tell the grandchildren family stories; we have family devotions and memorize Scripture so "the cousins" will remember learning these things together; we take lots of pictures; we play together, and we pray together.

God has told us stories. He has given us cherished keepsakes. There is a family history with celebrations and traditions that must be embraced and enjoyed by His family. There is a family treasure to discover and share. And there is plenty to go around. We don't have to squabble over this inheritance. In this economy, the more you give, the more you have.

---

∾

---

*Question:* Why is it important to teach the content of the covenant in the context of the covenant community?

*Answer:* Our covenant relationship with God must be reflected in our relationships with our Father's other adopted children for us to discover the full riches of our inheritance in Christ and for us to demonstrate to a watching world the reality of the Gospel of grace.

---

BECOMING A COVENANT-KEEPER

1.  Read Colossians 1 and reflect on the content and the context of the covenant. List the things you learn about Christ. Then list the evidences of covenant life among the people in Colosse. Remember that these evidences of covenant life are the result, not the cause, of their deliverance from the kingdom of darkness into the kingdom of light.

2. Memorize Colossians 2:2-3. Pray this for your church every day for a week. Then write your thoughts about the application of this verse to your church family.

3. Read Jesus' prayer for His covenant people in John 17. Is your life an answer to His prayer? Is the love among the covenant family in your church compelling evidence of the Gospel of grace?

4. Read the following verses and list the "family rules." Pray about your obedience to these commands. Pray about the corporate obedience of your church to these family rules. What are some ways your family, Sunday school class, or small group Bible study can obey these commands?

*Phil 2*

Romans 12:10, 13-18       Hebrews 3:13 *exhortation*
Romans 14:13, 19          1 Thessalonians 5:11-15
Romans 15:5-7             Hebrews 10:24-25 *love & good works*
Ephesians 4:2-3, 32       *gather together,*
Ephesians 5:21 *Submission*   James 4:11 *doer of the law (apply)*
James 5:9, 16, 19-20      1 Peter 4:8-10 *love one another*

*Restore one another in Christ*
*Pray for " "*

## CHRISTIAN EDUCATION IDEA

The Christian education committee can cultivate a sense of community by selecting a theme for the entire educational program of the church. Use a theme such as "Building God's Covenant Family" or "For Christ's Crown and Covenant." Also select a Scripture verse and a hymn to support the theme.

Write a purpose statement for the theme that clearly explains the vision and the strategy. For example:

The Christian education theme for the coming year will be "For Christ's Crown and Covenant." The theme verse is: "I heard a loud voice from the throne saying, 'Now the dwelling of God is with men, and he will live with them. They will be his people, and God himself will be with them and be their God'" (Revelation 21:3). The theme hymn is "Crown Him with Many Crowns."

Purpose: For our church to grow in our understanding of Christ's kingship and covenant, to celebrate our relationship with Him as His covenant people, and to authenticate this relationship by living covenantally with one another.

Strategy: The church year will begin with a series of sermons on Christ's Crown and Covenant. Each individual ministry in our educational program will determine at least one way to celebrate Christ's Crown and Covenant and one way to "maintain an holy fellowship" (*The Westminster Confession of Faith*, XXVI.2) by ministering to another group within our church family.

Have a planning session and ask the leadership of each individual ministry to come prepared to submit their plans for implementing the theme. It will be energizing for each group to hear the plans of other groups. As individual ideas are shared, the group will begin to get a vision for how the plans can be implemented and scheduled.

Throughout the year, use banners, bulletin boards, announcements, and testimonies to keep the theme before the congregation. A theme should not become just a slogan. It should be an educational tool. Events, publicity, and projects should have educational and theological integrity. For example, if the junior highs provide baby-sitting for the young adult class to have a party, teach the junior highs that this helps to "maintain an holy fellowship." If the women are planning a retreat, the publicity can explain that the purpose is for women to develop covenant relationships with one another.

The memory verse and hymn can be taught in classes and used in worship services. Families can be encouraged to use them in family worship. A book list for all ages can be suggested. These shared experiences will teach the content of the covenant while cultivating a context of community life.

# 3

*The Book
of the Covenant*

## LIVING AND TEACHING
## COVENANTALLY

### A SUNDAY SCHOOL TEACHER

When I was about twelve years old, my father became interested in a new Presbyterian church in Baltimore, Maryland. He decided that as many of his eight children as were living at home should attend the services with him. This was quite an undertaking, since the house where the church was meeting for its services was forty-five minutes from our home.

The Lord blessed this church with a good pastor and with Sunday school teachers who took a keen interest in their students. I was not a Christian at the time. My Sunday school teacher was Miss Wilhide, a middle-aged woman who insisted on teaching a class of boys ten to thirteen years old. She began every class with each boy offering a prayer to the Lord. Even though some of us didn't have much experience in praying, she would say, "If you don't think you know how to pray, I want you to say to the Lord, 'God be merciful to me, a sinner, and save me for Christ's sake.'" It took time, but many in the class came to understand what those words meant and became Christians.

The greatest impact Miss Wilhide had on my life was the way she took such an interest in me as one of her boys. The first summer I was in the church, our young people were encouraged to save money to go to camp. My family was poor, and there was no way I could go. Miss Wilhide became aware of my need and did an extraordinary thing. She took the little money she had and paid for me to go. You need to know that my dear teacher had no family to support her. She managed to scrape by through baby-sitting a few days a week. Though she had so little, she used what she had to bring about the miracle of our Lord's converting grace in my life. Her sacrifice that enabled me to go to camp actually changed my life and ultimately led to my going into the ministry and to the mission field.

Years later, while visiting a good friend who had also been one of Miss Wilhide's boys and who was then a seminary professor of Hebrew, he told me that she had made it possible for him to go on a retreat that changed his life. We were both amazed that this dear lady had made such an investment in our lives when we knew she had little money to give. But why should we have been surprised? The Scriptures say that God blesses the widow's mite so that her little accomplishes more than can be imagined.

Miss Wilhide lived alone and apparently had no relatives, but she gathered around her a group of boys whom she was able to influence with the Gospel. By God's grace, I was one of those boys, and I have thanked the Lord for her ever since.

—Robert Auffarth,
Newark, Delaware

# The Book of the Covenant

~

If the only effective way to teach the content of the covenant is in the context of covenant community, exactly how do we do this? Any *how-to* discussion should begin with the instruction manual. God has given us His book of the covenant. It is our authority. It is our rule for faith and practice.

The first three questions of *The Westminster Shorter Catechism* put the issue before us succinctly and clearly:

*1683 AD
· West. abbey*

Q. 1. What is the chief end of man?
A. Man's chief end is to glorify God, and to enjoy him for ever.

Q. 2. What rule hath God given to direct us how we may glorify and enjoy him?
A. The Word of God, which is contained in the Scriptures of the Old and New Testaments, is the only rule to direct us how we may glorify and enjoy him.

Q. 3. What do the Scriptures principally teach?
A. The Scriptures principally teach what man is to believe concerning God, and what duty God requires of man.

God's Word tells us what we are to believe and how we are to live. It is our rule because it is God's truth-message to us.

## KEEPER OF THE TRUTH

The church has been designated by God as the "pillar and foundation of truth" (1 Timothy 3:15). In commenting on this verse, Lewis Berkhof wrote:

The figure is expressive of the fact that the Church is the guardian of the truth, the citadel of the truth, and the defender of the truth over against all the enemies of the Kingdom of God. By giving His Word to the Church, God constituted the Church the keeper of the precious deposit of the truth. While hostile forces are pitted against it and the power of error is everywhere apparent, the Church must see to it that the truth does not perish from the earth, that the inspired volume in which it is embodied be kept pure and unmutilated, in order that its purpose may not be defeated, and that it be handed on faithfully from generation to generation. It has the great and responsible task of maintaining and defending the truth against all the forces of unbelief and error.[1]

John Calvin wrote:

We have laid down as distinguishing marks of the church the preaching of the Word and the observance of the sacraments. . . . It is of no small importance that it [the church] is called "the pillar and ground of the truth" and "the house of God" (1 Timothy 3:15). By these words Paul means that the church is the faithful keeper of God's truth in order that it may not perish in the world. For by its ministry and labor God willed to have the preaching of his Word kept pure and to show himself the Father of a family, while he feeds us with spiritual food and provides everything that makes for our salvation.[2]

A true church will purposefully keep, guard, and teach God's truth. Every effort must be taken to see that the church "correctly handles the word of truth" (2 Timothy 2:15) by teaching it in all its fullness. The Bible is not simply a disconnected collection of stories. It is God's revelation of Himself. It is His story of the redemption of His people.

In his book *Christ-Centered Preaching*, Dr. Bryan Chapell gives instruction to preachers that is applicable to all who want to understand and teach God's Word properly:

The redemptive dimension of a particular Scripture may not seem to dominate the text's landscape because the redemptive features of a passage sometimes appear only in seed form, just as revelation does. Still, to expose the revelation properly, we must see its redemptive content and context. We must relate even seed-form aspects of the text to the mature message they signal, or for which they prepare us, in order fully and rightly to interpret what the passage means. You do not explain what an acorn is, even if you say many true things about it (e.g., it is brown, has a cap, is found on the ground, is gathered by squirrels), if you do not in some way relate it to an oak tree. In a similar sense, preachers cannot properly explain biblical revelation, even if they say many true things about it, until they have related it to the redeeming work of God that all Scripture ultimately purposes to disclose.[3]

The church must not just teach about the acorns (people and events). The church must teach about the tree (redemption). It takes a covenantal perspective to do this.

## A COVENANTAL PERSPECTIVE OF SCRIPTURE

The Bible is a covenant document. It reveals the Initiator, the promise, and the terms of the covenant. Christianity is not simply a moral code. It is a covenant relationship with the living God. A relationship is impossible without knowledge.

In Scripture, God makes Himself known to His people. In the written Word, the living Word reveals Himself. This is why the psalmist wrote that God's Word revives the soul, makes the simple wise, gives joy to the heart and light to the eyes, and that it is more precious than gold and sweeter than honey (Psalm 19). This is why Paul could write to Timothy that the Scriptures could make him "wise for salvation through faith in Christ Jesus" and that "all Scripture is God-breathed and is useful for teaching, rebuking, correcting and training in righteousness, so that the man of God may be thoroughly equipped for every good work" (2 Timothy 3:15-17).

In Scripture, God teaches me about myself. I learn that my sinful tendencies are a manifestation of my sinful nature. I learn that my sin separates me from God's presence. I learn of my desperate need for a mediator to go before God on my behalf.

In Scripture, I learn that Jesus, the Mediator of the covenant, is the fulfillment of the "mother-promise" in Genesis 3:15. He is the Seed of the woman who crushed the head of the serpent so that we can live in God's presence. Jesus is the message of Scripture. We must see Him on every page of Scripture in order to understand God's message to us. It took the disciples awhile to understand this, but they finally saw.

## SLOW HEARTS . . . SAD HEARTS . . . BURNING HEARTS

On the third day after the crucifixion, two of the disciples were walking to Emmaus. They had heard the women's account of their visit to the tomb, but apparently put no stock in it because their hearts were sad. When the resurrected Jesus joined them, their faces were "downcast," and they did not recognize Him.

> *He asked them, "What are you discussing together as you walk along?" . . . One of them, named Cleopas, asked him, "Are you only a visitor to Jerusalem and do not know the things that have happened there in these days?"*
>
> *"What things?" he asked. "About Jesus of Nazareth," they replied. "He was a prophet, powerful in word and deed before God and all the people. The chief priests and our rulers handed him over to be sentenced to death, and they crucified him; but we had hoped that he was the one who was going to redeem Israel. And what is more, it is the third day since all this took place. In addition, some of our women amazed us. They went to the tomb early this morning but didn't find his body. They came and told us that they had seen a vision of angels, who*

*said he was alive. Then some of our companions went to the tomb and found it just as the women had said, but him they did not see."*

*He said to them, "How foolish you are, and how <u>slow of heart to believe</u> all that the prophets have spoken! Did not the Christ have to suffer these things and then enter his glory?"*

*And beginning with Moses and all the Prophets, he explained to them what was said in all the Scriptures concerning himself.*

*As they approached the village to which they were going, Jesus acted as if he were going farther. But they urged him strongly, "Stay with us, for it is nearly evening; the day is almost over." So he went in to stay with them.*

*When he was at the table with them, he took bread, gave thanks, broke it and began to give it to them. <u>Then their eyes were opened and they recognized him, and he disappeared from their sight.</u>*

*They asked each other, "Were not our hearts burning within us while he talked with us on the road and opened the Scriptures to us?"*

*They got up and returned at once to Jerusalem. There they found the Eleven and those with them, assembled together and saying, "It is true! The Lord has risen and has appeared to Simon."*

*Then the two told what had happened on the way, and how Jesus was recognized by them when he broke the bread.*

—Luke 24:17-35

The disciples had sad hearts because they had slow hearts. Hearts that are slow to believe God's Word quickly become downcast and discouraged. But their sa<u>d, slow hearts became burning hearts</u> when "beginning with Moses and all the Prophets, he explained to them what was said in all the Scriptures concerning himself."

When they saw Jesus on every page of Scripture, they were

transformed from lethargic, discouraged students to passionate, proclaiming heralds: "It is true! The Lord has risen. . . ."

## SHOW THEM JESUS

When we gather our students around us, we are to do the same thing Jesus did on the Emmaus road. We are to show them Jesus on every page of Scripture. It takes a covenantal perspective to do this.

It would be simplistic to say that there is one unifying principle of Scripture. Perhaps a better image would be to say that many beautiful threads are woven together to make the rope that ties it all together. Some of the threads we can follow are *presence*, or *dwelling of God*, or *covenant*, or *promise*, or *kingdom*. Whichever thread we unravel, it will point us to the same thing: Jesus. Scripture shows us Jesus. In our living and teaching, we are to do the same thing. We are to see and to show Jesus. When we do, God's covenant people will be transformed from lethargic, discouraged students susceptible to the lures of the culture to passionate heralds who proclaim that the promise is true—Jesus is alive.

A covenantal perspective of Scripture helps us see the tree (redemption), not just the acorns (the particular story). We must see the overarching message before we dip down to teach any individual part. If we "dip" without the rope, we may well drown in our own speculations about what it means. Simply telling the story of a person or an event is a superficial, fragmented view of Scripture and generally results in superficial, fragmented lives. This fragmentation usually carries us in one of three directions— legalism, liberalism, or moralism.

When we trivialize Scripture, we reduce the Christian life to formulas (legalism), or we rationalize away the demands (liberalism), or we concoct a list of things we are going to do for God (moralism). This eliminates the need for and the message of grace. A covenantal understanding points us to God's sovereign grace. This enables us to have a biblical world and life view so that we see ourselves and our lives from God's perspective. Let's use Genesis 12 as an example.

> *The LORD had said to Abram, "Leave your country, your people and your father's household and go to the land I will show you. I will make you into a great nation and I will bless you; I will make your name great, and you will be a blessing. I will bless those who bless you, and whoever curses you I will curse; and all peoples on earth will be blessed through you."*
>
> *So Abram left, as the LORD had told him; and Lot went with him. Abram was seventy-five years old when he set out from Haran. He took his wife Sarai, his nephew Lot, all the possessions they had accumulated and the people they had acquired in Haran, and they set out for the land of Canaan, and they arrived there. Abram traveled through the land as far as the site of the great tree of Moreh at Shechem. At that time the Canaanites were in the land.*
>
> *The LORD appeared to Abram and said, "To your offspring I will give this land." So he built an altar there to the LORD, who had appeared to him. From there he went on toward the hills east of Bethel and pitched his tent, with Bethel on the west and Ai on the east. There he built an altar to the LORD and called on the name of the LORD.*
>
> —Genesis 12:1-8

A superficial, fragmented approach tells the Abraham story and then hones in on Abraham's monumental step of faith. Abraham is held before us as a paragon of obedience, and the logic is that since he did it, I should do it. My response can go in one of the three directions mentioned above.

A *legalistic response* is that I will exert enormous effort trying to follow Abraham's example. I may even do foolish things such as tell my spouse I think we should move. I have no idea where we are to go, but it will be an Abraham-type step of faith if we do it. My rules for obedience make me feel very safe, and they will often become so entrenched in my thinking that I begin to impose them on others. If they are not following my formula, they are not being obedient.

A *liberal response* may be that I ponder the lesson of Abraham, conclude that radical obedience of that sort is not expected today, perhaps even seeing it as a fable, and dismiss the whole episode. I rationalize that it worked in that culture but has no application for today.

A *moralistic response* is that I look at Abraham, decide that I will live a life of radical obedience, and resolve to follow Jesus. My actions may well show that I am following through on my resolution. But the moral has been detached from the promise, and there is no change in my heart. It is self-effort rather than grace-power.

The first response makes me proud, the second response makes me comfortable, and the third response makes me tired. None of these is right. None confronts me with my need for grace and God's provision of grace.

A covenantal approach to Scripture begins with a desire for an Emmaus-road perspective. What does this passage say concerning Jesus? When God opens our spiritual eyes to see Jesus, our hearts will burn with a passion and a power to obey Him.

HOW TO DO IT

We must be focused and intentional as we read Scripture. We must look for Jesus on every page. The following questions can help to magnify our spiritual eyesight:

1.     What does this teach me about God's character and His promise?

2.     What does this teach me about Jesus, the Mediator of the covenant?

3.     What covenant privileges and responsibilities are mine because of who God is and what He has done and is doing for me through Jesus?

Reread Genesis 12 using these questions.

*What does this teach me about the character of God?* The starting point is God's revelation of Himself. He is showing us Himself so

Covenant: Land - Canaan/Heaven
Seed - Children
Blessing - Christ

we can know Him and have a relationship with Him. In this passage we learn that He came to Abraham and called him by name. He initiated the relationship with Abraham just as He had done with Adam. He is a personal God who speaks and who makes promises. When He initiated the relationship with Abraham, He made Himself known as the LORD, or Yahweh. This name "proclaimed His eternal, self-sustaining, self-determining, sovereign reality. . . ."[4] This is His personal name that signifies a covenant relationship with Him. When He revealed Himself to Abraham as Yahweh, this was a preincarnate appearance of Jesus Christ. He revealed His character and His covenant, so Abraham knew that the promise and the demand were credible.

*What does this teach me about Jesus, the Mediator of the covenant?* When Yahweh said that all peoples on the planet would be blessed through him, Abraham saw Jesus, and his heart burned with zeal to obey. Abraham was fully aware that he was no better and no smarter than any of the other pagans in Ur. He deserved nothing. But Yahweh came, He called him by name, and He told him of the promised Seed who would make possible the blessing of living in His presence.

*What covenant privileges and responsibilities are mine because of who God is and what He has done and is doing for me through Jesus?* Abraham's response was not a reflection of his own virtuous character. His response was based solely on the character of the one who made the promise. Without question or hesitation Abraham left, he took his family, and he built an altar. Herein is the essence of a covenant-keeper—separation from our old way of life, worshiping God, and assuming our corporate responsibilities.

The beauty of this extraordinary encounter is not Abraham's response. The splendor of this divine appointment is that Yahweh revealed Himself and His covenant promise to the creature of His hand. Sovereign grace is irresistible. When we see Jesus as He reveals Himself in Scripture, our hearts are wooed and won by His love. We, like Abraham and the disciples, will become passionate heralds of the Gospel.

In *Promise and Deliverance*, S. G. DeGraaf explains how to tell the stories of Bible history. He uses the words *story* and *history* interchangeably.

> I object to the idea that the children will not remember any-
> thing unless some particular Bible personality is made the
> midpoint of the story being told. Little children, according to
> the usual line of argument, have to learn to identify with a
> particular person in the story. But that person, with *his* acts
> and *his* faith and *his* mistakes, then becomes the central fig-
> ure. When we take this step, the story we tell is no longer the
> history of revelation. I must admit that it is very difficult to
> tell the stories in the proper way. It is difficult enough to see
> things this way in our own minds. First we must subject our-
> selves to the Scriptures and their meaning. Learning to listen
> carefully to the Scripture passage we are studying will cost
> us a couple of hours of preparation (or perhaps more), but
> what else can we do? We have no choice, for we are dealing
> with Scripture! If we are not determined to tell of God first
> and last, of God as the Alpha and the Omega, we should not
> even bother telling the Bible story.[5]

## DEVELOPING A BIBLICAL WORLDVIEW

Teaching covenantally equips students to think biblically. When they look beyond the person or event and see Jesus, they encounter the person of God, and they begin to fathom His covenant promise to live in relationship with us. They begin to see that this covenant is sovereignly initiated and sovereignly sustained. As they begin to comprehend the marvelous sovereignty of God, they begin think-ing integratively. All of their thoughts about faith and life begin to coalesce around the person of Jesus. A biblical worldview starts to take shape. Their hearts burn to integrate Jesus into every sphere of life and to proclaim the majesty of the sovereign King who promised to be our God and to live among us.

Abraham Kuyper made one of the classic definitive statements about a biblical worldview. According to Richard J. Mouw, in his book *Uncommon Decency,*

> Abraham Kuyper, who lived from 1837 to 1920, founded a Christian political party, and he even served as prime minister of the Netherlands during the early years of the twentieth century. He was also a gifted philosopher-theologian, a well-known educator, and a prolific journalist. And Abraham Kuyper was an ardent Calvinist who believed passionately in the sovereignty of God. . . . He insisted that God wants Christians to be active in *showing forth* the divine rule. Jesus is King, and we are his subjects. This means that we must try to be obedient to the reign of Jesus in all areas of our lives: family relationships, friendships, business, politics, leisure time, art, science, farming. In whatever we do, we must seek to glorify God. My favorite Kuyper quotation comes from a speech that he once gave before a university audience in Amsterdam. He was arguing that scholarship is an important form of Christian discipleship. Since scholarship deals with God's world, it has to be done in such a way that it honors Christ. Kuyper concluded with this ringing proclamation: "There is not one square inch of the entire creation about which Jesus Christ does not cry out, 'This is mine! This belongs to me!'"
>
> When Kuyper pictured Jesus as crying out that everything in the universe belongs to him, he was not suggesting that the Lord is a self-centered property owner. Jesus isn't like a toddler who screeches, "Mine!" as he yanks toys away from his playmates. Kuyper knew that for Jesus, "This is mine!" expresses a love so deep that he was willing to suffer and die in order to rescue his creation from sin.[6]

A biblical worldview compels our students to engage culture and claim the crown rights of the King of Glory. They will move into government, education, business, the arts, and all other arenas and declare, "This belongs to King Jesus."

COMMUNITY IMPLICATIONS

Some of the most splendid moments in Israel's history were those times when the community renewed their covenant obligations before the Lord. One of these occurred during the reign of Josiah. He was only eight years old when he became king, but "he did what was right in the eyes of the LORD and walked in the ways of his father David, not turning aside to the right or to the left. In the eighth year of his reign, while he was still young, he began to seek the God of his father David" (2 Chronicles 34:2-3).

Josiah carried out extensive reforms, including the restoration of the temple. When Hilkiah the high priest found the "Book of the Law of the LORD that had been given through Moses" (vs. 14), he sent it to the king. The scroll, probably Deuteronomy, was read to the king, and he tore his robes as a sign of his remorse and repentance. He immediately summoned his attendants: "Go and inquire of the LORD for me and for the remnant in Israel and Judah about what is written in this book that has been found. Great is the Lord's anger that is poured out on us because our fathers have not kept the word of the LORD; they have not acted in accordance with all that is written in this book" (vs. 21).

The attendants went to the prophetess Huldah, who said to them:

*This is what the LORD, the God of Israel, says: "Tell the man who sent you to me, 'This is what the LORD says: I am going to bring disaster on this place and its people—all the curses written in the book that has been read in the presence of the king of Judah. Because they have forsaken me and burned incense to other gods and provoked me to anger by all that their hands have made, my anger will be poured out on this place and will not be quenched. . . . Because your heart was responsive and you humbled yourself before God when you heard what he spoke against this place and its people, and because you humbled yourself before me and tore your robes and wept in my presence, I have heard you, declares the LORD. Now I will gather you to your fathers, and you will be buried in peace. Your eyes will not see all the disaster I am going to bring on this place and on those who live here.'"*

—*2 Chronicles 34:23-28*

Disaster would come on the nation, but the king would be spared. Josiah could have sighed with relief and considered the case closed, but Josiah understood his community responsibility.

*Then the king called together all the elders of Judah and Jerusalem. He went up to the temple of the LORD with the men of Judah, the people of Jerusalem, the priests and the Levites—all the people from the least to the greatest. He read in their hearing all the words of the Book of the Covenant, which had been found in the temple of the LORD. The king stood by his pillar and renewed the covenant in the presence of the LORD—to follow the LORD and keep his commands, regulations and decrees with all his heart and all his soul, and to obey the words of the covenant written in this book. Then he had everyone in Jerusalem and Benjamin pledge themselves to it; the people of Jerusalem did this in accordance with the covenant of God, the God of their fathers. Josiah removed all the detestable idols from all the territory belonging to the Israelites, and he had all who were present in Israel serve the LORD their God. As long as he lived, they did not fail to follow the LORD, the God of their fathers.*

—*2 Chronicles 34:29-33*

Then Josiah led the people in a national celebration of the Passover in Jerusalem, and he reinstituted proper worship.

*He appointed the priests to their duties and encouraged them in the service of the Lord's temple.*

—*2 Chronicles 35:2*

Josiah's leadership was bold and brilliant, but the stimulus for this national renewal was the discovery of God's Word. When the people gathered around God's Word and submitted to its authority, there was unity and reformation.

In a sense, on every Lord's Day God's people should gather around His Word and enter into a community celebration of the covenant promise and a community renewal of covenant responsibilities. In Romans 15:1-13, Paul gives us a glimpse of what this will look like.

> *We who are strong ought to bear with the failings of the weak and not to please ourselves. Each of us should please his neighbor for his good, to build him up. For even Christ did not please himself but, as it is written: "The insults of those who insult you have fallen on me." For everything that was written in the past was written to teach us, so that through endurance and the encouragement of the Scriptures we might have hope.*
>
> *May the God who gives endurance and encouragement give you a spirit of unity among yourselves as you follow Christ Jesus, so that with one heart and mouth you may glorify the God and Father of our Lord Jesus Christ.*
>
> *Accept one another, then, just as Christ accepted you, in order to bring praise to God. For I tell you that Christ has become a servant of the Jews on behalf of God's truth, to confirm the promises made to the patriarchs so that the Gentiles may glorify God for his mercy, as it is written: "Therefore I will praise you among the Gentiles; I will sing hymns to your name."*
>
> *Again, it says, "Rejoice, O Gentiles, with his people."*
>
> *And again, "Praise the Lord, all you Gentiles, and sing praises to him, all you peoples."*
>
> *And again, Isaiah says, "The Root of Jesse will spring up, one who will arise to rule over the nations; the Gentiles will hope in him."*
>
> *May the God of hope fill you with all joy and peace as you trust in him, so that you may overflow with hope by the power of the Holy Spirit.*

These commands to bear with the failings of the weak, to please our neighbors and build them up, and to accept one another, are not flimsy platitudes. This is not an attempt to manufacture an artificial unity that makes us feel better. These commands are impossible. They drive us to acknowledge our need for grace. Jesus is the promise, the pattern, and the power, and "everything that was written in the past was written to teach us, so that through endurance and the encouragement of the Scriptures we might have hope." They drove Paul to pray that "the God of hope fill you with all joy and peace as you trust in him, so that you may overflow with hope by the power of the Holy Spirit."

The King of Glory accepts me, and He has given His Word and His Spirit to teach me, to encourage me, and to empower me to accept His other children in such a profound way that our hearts will beat as one and our voices sound as one. When we are centered on seeing Jesus on every page of Scripture, our unity in Him and our praise of Him will converge in a doxology to the praise of His Crown and Covenant.

TAKE-AWAY POINT

A careless, slipshod approach to Scripture results in a sloppy approach to obedience. Seeing people and events in Scripture as examples to follow rather than seeing Jesus will cause us and our students to be downcast and discouraged. Paul challenged Timothy to "do your best to present yourself to God as one approved, a workman who does not need to be ashamed and who correctly handles the word of truth" (2 Timothy 2:15). This is also his challenge to us. We must do it for the honor of Christ's Crown and Covenant.

---

∞

---

*Question:* What is a covenantal perspective of Scripture?

*Answer:* A covenantal perspective means that we see Scripture as God's revelation of Himself, of His covenant promise to redeem a people, and of His provision to keep

His promise. We must look for this redemptive dimension. We must look for Jesus on every page of Scripture. Our knowledge of God's character and His promise determines our view of our lives and the world.

---

### BECOMING A COVENANT-KEEPER

1. Write a brief summary statement for the following:
   Why does a covenantal approach help students think biblically and develop a biblical worldview?

2. Read Psalm 19 and list the ways God's Word is described and the things God's Word does for us.

3. Read Romans 15:1-7. Write a prayer for your church based on this passage.

### CHRISTIAN EDUCATION IDEA

A church-wide Scripture memory program will help God's people hide His Word in their hearts (Psalm 119:11), and it can "gather" a church around selected portions of the Word.

One approach for a Scripture memory program is a list of verses for each age.[7] More verses are covered with this method, but it may be difficult for a church to develop a program to sustain this approach.

Another approach is for people of all ages to learn the same verses. This is easier to manage, families can work on the memory verses together, and it promotes unity between various age-groups. This program can be done on a three-year cycle. Children may repeat verses, but doing so will reinforce and expand their memorization and understanding of the verses. Here are some ideas for developing this program.

•Compile a list of verses. Send the list to all parents. Have a definite time frame, perhaps September through May. You could have another list for the summer.

•Use one of the children's programs to teach the meaning of the verses and to recite the verses with the children. This could be a Sunday school assembly for all children or a weekday Bible club.

•Encourage older children to help younger children learn the verses.

•Have a designated time when children can recite. Involve teens by using them as listeners. Have a sheet for each child with the list of verses so that the listener can record the date the verse was recited. Add interest by giving a "memory verse bead" for each verse that is recited. The beads can be strung on leather string.

•Divide the verses into two parts. Tell the children that there will be a special event in January for everyone who has recited all of the verses in the first section. Then plan another event in May for everyone who completes the memory work.

•Periodically have the children recite the verses in a worship service.

I had the great joy of seeing an eleven-year-old girl sit with a six-year-old boy at a family night supper so that she could help him prepare to recite a verse. She was then given a "character bead" during the assembly for her leadership in helping a younger member of our church family.

# 4

*Home
and Church*

## LIVING AND TEACHING
## COVENANTALLY

### A HOME AND A CHURCH

I am a covenant child. According to the Scriptures, that in itself should indicate what my life and spiritual pilgrimage have been like. Truly, I am among all people most blessed.

I am the child of Christian parents, Christian grandparents, and Christian great-grandparents. Like Timothy, I have been taught God's Word since infancy. And, as Moses commanded, I was taught at the table, on the road, in my bed, and everywhere in between. I can't remember a time when I did not know that God loved me and that the Lord Jesus died for me and that we were therefore obviously to love and obey Him in return.

My older brother, with seven-year-old evangelistic zeal, asked Jesus into *my* heart when I was four. The following year I was having a heart-to-heart with Daddy as he was tucking me in bed and hearing my prayers. He explained that God loved me more even than he did and that I needed God even more than I needed him. I knelt with Daddy that night and told my heavenly Father that my life was His.

But this is not all. I am a covenant child—which means that I am also a child of the church. When an infant is baptized, the congregation affirms that they will all be godparents to the baby. My congregation took their vow quite seriously. I had more surrogate moms, dads, grandmoms, and granddads than I knew what to do with, and they lovingly tended me as one of their own. Psalm 92:13 tells us that children planted in God's house will flourish, and flourish I did. We are told that we must come to the kingdom as a little child, so what a blessing for me to come as a child—understanding from the first what it means to be a child of the King.

My simple but genuine faith was carefully cultivated by my godly parents and shepherding church, both giving faithful instruction. I have not struggled significantly with doubting God's truth, because I have been surrounded by living examples of His love and obedience to His Word in all walks of life.

Considering these abundant blessings, my sanctification has been shamefully slow. But I am His, and He will finish what He started. So many people in our sad times are striving to overcome their past, but I cling to my heritage as my greatest treasure. Our Lord has ordained praise from the lips of small children like me. I pray that my life will be a doxology to the praise of His glorious grace.

—Paige Benton,
Nashville, Tennessee

# Home
# and Church

∾

We live in a broken culture that is grasping for a sense of direction by talking about family values and about governmental villages raising our children. When Christians frantically try to protect their families by embracing these cultural notions, we risk making idols of the family and the government. Christian families do not exist in isolation from one another. Each Christian family should be a snapshot of God's kingdom values, but the church is the mural. The church, the covenant community, is to be the compelling panorama of grace.

The home and church must work together to teach the covenant way of life. There are many excellent books on the Christian home and on body life in the church. And there are many aspects of church and family life that are of utmost importance. This chapter has the limited purpose of discussing one aspect, the relationship between the home and church, and the relevance of that relationship in contextualizing the covenant.

## DEVASTATING DISTINCTION

To differentiate between family values and kingdom values is a devastating distinction because it undermines the essence of the covenant community and the strength of the Christian home. The balance between home and church is delicate. It is easy to lose our equilibrium and drift off-center.

Some drift towards a casual approach to church attendance. This is heard in comments such as:

"We missed church on Sunday because we needed a family outing. It was a beautiful day so we went on a picnic."

"We haven't found a church we like, and anyway our family prefers watching a worship service on television and then going out for brunch."

"We can't attend Sunday night worship because that is our family time."

This approach seems to forget God's command to "remember the Sabbath day by keeping it holy" (Exodus 20:8). It forgets His promise that "if you keep your feet from breaking the Sabbath and from doing as you please on my holy day, if you call the Sabbath a delight and the LORD's holy day honorable, and if you honor it by not going your own way and not doing as you please or speaking idle words, then you will find your joy in the LORD, and I will cause you to ride on the heights of the land and to feast on the inheritance of your father Jacob" (Isaiah 58:13-14). It forgets the family rule that says, "Let us not give up meeting together, as some are in the habit of doing, but let us encourage one another—and all the more as you see the Day approaching" (Hebrews 10:25).

This approach minimizes the value of families worshiping together. Worshiping and serving the God of glory together is the best quality time families can possibly spend.

On the other end of the spectrum are those who make a list of rules and methods they believe everyone in the community must follow. The rules make them feel secure, and soon the rules become an idol. When a community environment develops where everyone dresses alike, follows the same dietary regimen, uses the same child-rearing methods, educates their children the same way, and assumes that those who make other choices are not spiritual, there is no unity because there is no diversity. It is boring and oppressive sameness. There is no need for grace. You simply fall in line and follow the leader.

Maintaining family/church balance is not a one-time decision. It is the ongoing process of sanctification. We won't get it exactly right until we get to heaven. We will make huge blunders along the way. But we must keep trying for the sake of Christ's Crown and Covenant. The family-church mural will be marred unless the family and church continually pray for wisdom to understand our responsibility before God and to one another.

## FAMILY RESPONSIBILITY TO THE COMMUNITY

In the Old Testament, a family priority was their corporate identity as the people of God. God told them that they were to "camp around the Tent of Meeting some distance from it, each man under his standard with the banners of his family" (Numbers 2:2). The arrangement of their tents caused them to face the tabernacle, the visible representation of God's presence among them. As they faced the Presence, they also faced one another. ". . . That is the way they encamped under their standards, and that is the way they set out, each with his clan and family" (Numbers 2:34). As each family marched forward under their banner, there was both family and community identity, solidarity, and safety. Any family who broke rank was weak and vulnerable.

In this discussion of family responsibilities regarding church life, I will switch from writing to reporting. I defer to two godly men.

J. C. Ryle, an Anglican bishop of the nineteenth century, in a little booklet entitled *The Duties of Parents*, wrote:

> Tell them [your children] of the duty and privilege of going to the house of God, and joining in the prayers of the congregation. Tell them that wherever the Lord's people are gathered together, there the Lord Jesus is present in an especial manner, and that those who absent themselves must expect, like the Apostle Thomas, to miss a blessing. Tell them of the importance of hearing the Word preached, and that it is God's ordinance for converting, sanctifying, and building up the souls of men. Tell them how the Apostle Paul enjoins us not "to forsake the assembling of ourselves together, as the manner of some is" (Heb. 10:25); but to exhort one another, to stir one

another up to it, and so much the more as we see the day approaching. . . .

Do not allow them to grow up with a habit of making vain excuses for not coming. Give them plainly to understand, that so long as they are under your roof, it is the rule of your house for everyone in health to honour the Lord's house upon the Lord's day, and that you reckon the Sabbath-breaker to be a murderer of his own soul.

See to it too, if it can be so arranged, that your children go with you to church and sit near you when they are there. To go to church is one thing, but to behave well at church is quite another. And believe me, there is no security for good behaviour like that of having them under your own eye.[1]

George Grant, a godly father and teacher of our generation, writes:

Our children depend not only on good marriages and caring homes for their health and well-being, but on sound churches as well. Our cultural agenda must not simply be one more conservative, deregulated, traditional-virtues, and community-based program. It must be forthrightly biblical. It must be rooted, not simply in family values, but in kingdom values. Children need good news. They need the Good News. . . .

We must immerse them in the life of the community of faith. We must provide them with all the blessings of the covenant. And that is a task that transcends mere hearth and home.

The church has the keys to the kingdom (Matt. 16:19), the power to bind and loose (Matt. 18:18). It will prevail over the very gates of hell (Matt. 16:18). It offers the Waters of Life (Rev. 22:17), the Bread of Life (John 6:35), and the Word of Life (John 1:1), because its Head is the Author of Life (Acts 17:25).

Our children need kingdom values no less than family values. And to that end, in the good providence of God, the church is *Plan A*. There is no *Plan B*.[2]

Christian parents have a high privilege and responsibility to "immerse their children in the life of the community of faith" and to cultivate in them a sense of family and community identity and solidarity.

## CHURCH'S RESPONSIBILITY TO FAMILIES

A word of caution is in order before beginning this discussion. In the last chapter we saw that the marks of a true church are the faithful preaching and teaching of God's Word and the proper administration of the sacraments. The issues discussed in this chapter are not essentials to the essence of a church. They are, however, evidences that the members of the church are applying God's Word in their lives. So as we discuss these issues, none of us should point a finger at our church and say, "They don't do that." We are "they." Every issue raised in this section should cause me to examine my own heart and life as a member of the community.

As "the keeper of God's truth," the church is responsible to teach that truth to God's children. Building on the foundation of God's Word, church members must carefully consider the relationship between the home and church. They must carefully cultivate a community of faith where Christian parents can joyfully immerse their children in the community life. There is no formula for doing this. Many things should be considered. It will look different in different churches. The following are simply some basic starting points. There must be an ongoing, lively discussion for each local church to work this out in its situation.

First, any attempt to live covenantally must be undergirded with fervent prayer. In *A Call to Prayer: An Urgent Plea to Enter into the Secret Place*, J. C. Ryle wrote:

> I commend to you the importance of intercession in our prayers. We are all selfish by nature, and our selfishness is very apt to stick to us, even when we are converted. There is a tendency in us to think only of our own souls, our own spir-

itual conflicts, our own progress in religion, and to forget others. Against this tendency we all have need to watch and strive, and not least in our prayers. We should study to be of a public spirit. We should stir ourselves up to name other names besides our own before the throne of grace. We should try to bear in our hearts the whole world, the heathen . . . the body of true believers, the professing Protestant churches, the country in which we live, the congregation to which we belong, the household in which we sojourn, the friends and relations we are connected with. For each and all of these we should plead. This is the highest charity. He loves me best who loves me in his prayers. This is for our soul's health. It enlarges our sympathies and expands our hearts. This is for the benefit of the church. The wheels of all machinery for extending the gospel are moved by prayer. They do as much for the Lord's cause who intercede like Moses on the mount as they do who fight like Joshua in the thick of the battle. This is to be like Christ. He bears the names of his people, as their High Priest, before the Father. Oh, the privilege of being like Jesus! This is to be a true helper to ministers. If I must choose a congregation, give me a people that pray.[3]

Second, church leadership must be committed to the content of the covenant and to covenant life in the church. Everything that has been discussed in the previous chapters should be taught to the church family. The preaching and teaching ministry should be intentional in teaching the biblical basis for community life.

Third, the relationships of church leaders, including all teachers, should model this covenantal life in such a way that an atmosphere is created where God's people are encouraged in heart and united in love. It should be an inclusive community where infants, children, teens, and adults of all ages are valued as members of the family.

Fourth, there should be continual teaching and discussions about harmonizing unity and diversity. Paul's prayer for the church in Rome must become the prayer and practice of each church. "May the God who gives endurance and encouragement give you a spirit of unity among yourselves as you follow Christ Jesus, so that with one heart and mouth you may glorify the God and Father of our Lord Jesus Christ. Accept one another, then, just as Christ accepted you, in order to bring praise to God" (Romans 15:5-7). There must be an attitude of acceptance that allows for our individual preferences and our various levels of spiritual maturity.

Fifth, there must be built-in mechanisms to teach and prepare people to handle conflicts, crises, disappointments, and ambivalent feelings about the church. Members of the church family should be taught how to mourn with those who mourn, where to turn in times of crisis, biblical principles to deal with conflict, and appropriate responses to disappointments. They should know the procedures for getting financial aid from the church or counseling about marriage difficulties. Crisis and conflict are times of such intensity that it is often difficult to act rationally. Teaching people what to do during these times will fortify them to withstand the temptation to become discouraged and abandon the church.

Sixth, repentance and forgiveness must be taught and modeled. God's people must understand the absolute necessity of praying for repenting grace and forgiving grace in our relationships with one another.

Seventh, there should be frequent family celebrations and traditions so that the community learns to rejoice with those who rejoice. Weddings, baby showers, anniversaries, corporate prayer for specific needs, calling the elders to pray for the sick, testimonies of answered prayer, and expressions of appreciation for help received from the community will help the community to "maintain an holy fellowship."

Eighth, there should be opportunities for people of all ages to be involved in ministries of mercy. It is not sufficient to tell God's people to be compassionate. They should be mobilized to show compassion to the poor, the afflicted, the lonely, the hurting. There should be opportunities for mission trips, outreach to international students, tutoring programs, ministries to the physically and mentally handicapped, and care for the sick, elderly, lonely and oppressed.

Ninth, a high commitment must be placed on the church's responsibility to covenant children. This, of course, raises the question:

## WHAT IS A COVENANT CHILD?

There is a twofold answer to this question.

*Answer #1:*

The first part of the answer is that a covenant child is the child of at least one believing parent. "For the unbelieving husband has been sanctified through his wife, and the unbelieving wife has been sanctified through her believing husband. Otherwise your children would be unclean, but as it is, they are holy" (1 Corinthians 7:14).

Charles Hodge wrote:

> In the sight of God parents and children are one. The former are the authorized representatives of the latter; they act for them; they contract obligations in their name. In all cases, therefore, where parents enter into covenant with God, they bring their children with them. . . . If a man joined the commonwealth of Israel, he secured for his children the benefits of the theocracy, unless they willingly renounced them. And so when a believer adopts the covenant of grace, he brings his children within that covenant, in the sense that God promises to give them, in his own good time, all the benefits of redemption, provided they do not willingly renounce their baptismal engagements.[4]

Covenant children are entitled to certain benefits of the covenant. These benefits include hearing God's Word in the context of loving relationships in the home and church, prayer, and the blessed privilege of growing up as a part of the community of faith as he/she participates in church life from infancy.

Obviously this is not a guarantee that every child of every

Christian parent is automatically saved. But it does mean that because of the covenant relationship God has with believers, He works in a covenantal way in the lives of their children. The promises are undeniable:

*As for me, this is my covenant with you: You will be the father of many nations. . . . I will make you very fruitful; I will make nations of you, and kings will come from you. I will establish my covenant as an everlasting covenant between me and you and your descendants after you for the generations to come, to be your God and the God of your descendants after you.*

*—Genesis 17:4, 6-7*

*Know therefore that the LORD your God is God; he is the faithful God, keeping his covenant of love to a thousand generations of those who love him and keep his commands.*

*—Deuteronomy 7:9*

*The children of your servants will live in your presence; their descendants will be established before you.*

*—Psalm 102:28*

*But from everlasting to everlasting the LORD's love is with those who fear him, and his righteousness with their children's children—with those who keep his covenant and remember to obey his precepts.*

*—Psalm 103:17-18*

*"As for me, this is my covenant with them" says the LORD. "My Spirit, who is on you, and my words that I have put in your mouth will not depart from your mouth, or from the mouths of your children, or from the mouths of their descendants from this time on and forever," says the LORD.*

*—Isaiah 59:21*

*My servant David will be king over them, and they will all have one shepherd. They will follow my laws and be careful to keep my decrees. They will live in the land I gave to my servant Jacob, the land where your fathers lived. They and their children and their children's children will live there forever, and David my servant will be their prince forever. I will make a covenant of peace with them; it will be an everlasting covenant. I will establish them and increase their numbers, and I will put my sanctuary among them forever. My dwelling place will be with them; I will be their God, and they will be my people.*

—Ezekiel 37:24-27

*The promise is for you and your children and for all who are far off—or all whom the LORD our God will call.*

—Acts 2:39

However, the responsibility is also undeniable.

Parents and grandparents are commanded to "be careful, and watch yourselves closely so that you do not forget the things your eyes have seen or let them slip from your heart as long as you live. Teach them to your children and to their children after them" (Deuteronomy 4:9).

Fathers are commanded to bring their children up in the "training and instruction of the Lord" (Ephesians 6:4).

Children are responsible to "believe in the Lord Jesus Christ, and you will be saved" (Acts 16:31). Each child must ratify the covenant by embracing Jesus as his Savior. This may not be a specific event whereby the child can recall the moment of conversion. A "Timothy testimony" of knowing the Scriptures from infancy (2 Timothy 3:14) is normative for a covenant child. But it must be personal. He cannot ride into heaven on the covenant coattails of his parents. God does not have grandchildren.

Covenant children have a special place within the church. They are to be taught that they are members of God's covenant family, that they have responsibilities within that family, and that the family of God has responsibilities concerning them.

*Answer #2:*

What about the neighbor child who goes to church with your family while his own parents sleep in on Sunday morning? What about the myriad of first-generation Christians who did not grow up in Christian homes? Are they second-class citizens of the kingdom because they were not born into Christian homes? Where do they fit in?

Several years after his initial encounter with Yahweh, Abraham was still childless. How could God keep His promise when there was no heir and the biological clock had stopped ticking? "Then the word of the LORD came to him: '. . . a son coming from your own body will be your heir.' He took him outside and said, 'Look up at the heavens and count the stars—if indeed you can count them.' Then he said to him, 'So shall your offspring be'" (Genesis 15:4-5).

Abraham's offspring are covenant children. Who are Abraham's children? "If you belong to Christ, then you are Abraham's seed, and heirs according to the promise" (Galatians 3:29). So the second part of the answer is that in the broad sense, all believers are children of the covenant.

Peter gave this twofold answer at the conclusion of his sermon on the day of Pentecost. He preached covenantally to the thousands assembled before him. He showed them Jesus in the Old Testament. And their hearts were pricked. "When the people heard this, they were cut to the heart and said to Peter and the other apostles, 'Brothers, what shall we do?'"

Peter didn't skip a beat. Even with this colossal church growth opportunity, his covenantal church growth strategy did not waver. "Repent and be baptized, every one of you, in the name of Jesus Christ for the forgiveness of your sins. And you will receive the gift of the Holy Spirit. The promise is for you and your children and for all who are far off—for all whom the Lord our God will call" (Acts 2:37-39).

His first line of offense in a continuing kingdom advancement was the children of believers. "The promise is for you and your children . . ." But he did not stop there: ". . . and for all who are far off—for all whom the Lord our God will call."

## PRESENTING THE GOSPEL TO COVENANT CHILDREN

Sometimes parents and teachers are unsure about how to present the Gospel to little children. First, it is important to remember that little children can know the Lord Jesus Christ as their Savior. The Holy Spirit's work is not limited by age. God applies the message of salvation to whomever He chooses whenever He chooses.

In presenting the Gospel to covenant children, we must realize that for some there is a definite time and place when they repent of their sins and turn in faith to Jesus Christ, while there are others who never remember a time when they did not love Jesus. The important thing is not an instantaneous experience but rather signs of regeneration such as a love for God, a desire to hear His Word, a loving and obedient attitude, a love for others, and a growth in holiness.

At the same time, we must not neglect our responsibility to teach them what a Christian is and how one becomes a Christian. We believe this will be done naturally as you help children understand the Bible and how it applies to their lives, and as they see the reality of Christ in the lives of the adults around them.

Though normally covenant children grow into salvation by gradual nurture and training, we should be sensitive to key opportunities to instruct them in how to ask for forgiveness of sin and how to exercise their faith in Jesus Christ. Do not be hesitant to pray with a little child who says, "I want to become a Christian," or "I want Jesus in my heart." The child may not fully understand all of the implications, but neither did we. That understanding will grow.

Since faith and understanding are interrelated, our growth in the Christian life is a process.

When teaching children who are not from Christian homes, we must remember that God has brought these children to us, and they also should be taught that they need to have their sins forgiven and to trust in Jesus. However, knowing the implications and the blessings of the covenant, our greatest responsibility to these children may be to reach out to them and their parents with the good news of Jesus Christ. Our sincere love for and interest in a child may provide a wonderful opportunity to share the Gospel with the parents.

Jesus said, "Let the little children come to me, and do not hinder them . . ." (Matthew 19:14). We let them come by teaching them God's Word in the context of a covenant community that authenticates the Word.

### Answer #1 Example

Charles and Laura Joseph are covenant children who now have children of their own. They want their children to have the faith perspective that has been passed on to them and the covenant community life experience that has shaped them. Their faith perspective was shaken but not destroyed during Laura's first pregnancy. She was carrying twins, and it was a high-risk pregnancy. Blake and Brannon were born prematurely, and there were complications. Brannon was affected most severely with physical and mental handicaps. The doctors did not think he would ever walk. Through much prayer and perseverance, he finally began walking at three and a half.

When Charles and Laura shared their testimony in a young adult Sunday school class, their delight in their four children was obvious. They expressed confidence that all of their children, including Brannon, are exactly as God created them for His purposes. They do not doubt God's sovereign love in their lives. As part of their testimony, they had been asked to tell how the church can minister to special-needs children and their parents. Charles's answer was profound in its simplicity.

"When Brannon was two years old, he was still crawling. Despite his size and uncoordinated movements, the nursery volunteers treated him just as they did all the other babies. They cuddled and rocked him. They made him feel special. They loved him. This is what special-needs children need. This is what every child needs."

This is what every adult can do. This is what every adult must do if we are going to teach our children the covenant way of life so that they will never want to renounce their place in the covenant family.

The twins are now ten years old. One of Brannon's greatest delights is singing in the children's choir. Though he cannot always stand still and his arms sometimes make awkward motions, the other children in the choir and the adults who watch find great delight in this covenant child. He is a special gift to our church.

### Answer #2 Example

The women of Covenant Presbyterian Church in Waynesville, North Carolina, range in age from sixty-two to eighty-five. By the mid-1980s, most of the church's children had grown and scattered. But these women believed there were children who needed the truth of the covenant in their Blue Ridge Mountain community, so they went searching for them. They looked for children without Christ, without love, and without adequate food and clothing. Their hearts began to yearn for these children. They searched the harvest fields and soon located a group of tenant houses on the outskirts of Waynesville. They visited, and they loved. They developed a teaching and enrichment ministry for the children that includes Sunday school, children's church, and Vacation Bible School; literacy classes to aid their learning abilities and homework skills; musical enrichment with several children being taught to play the piano, harp, and violin; and provision for physical needs such as clothing.

These women set their spiritual sights on those "who are far off—for all whom the Lord our God will call" (Acts 2:39), and they have lifted high the banner of Christ's Crown and Covenant.

### THE COMMUNITY BANNER

Christ's Crown and Covenant is our banner. If we rally under anything less, our unity is precarious. Our individual family banners may look somewhat different. Some may be shocking pink and others a subdued beige. Some may be precisely designed and constructed while others are a hilarious hodgepodge. Some are brand-new, and others are tattered and torn. But regardless of the size, shape, and color, they all proclaim the same glorious message. When we put them all together, they declare the wonder of God's glory and our uncompromising commitment to reflect His glory. We must remember that the world will be diverted from that declaration if we even hint that we think some banners are better or more beautiful than others. Community solidarity strengthens and protects each individual family and glorifies the King of the church.

### TAKE-AWAY POINT

Amy Carmichael, an Irish missionary, spent fifty-three years in India without a furlough. She founded the Dohnavur Fellowship, a refuge for children. Her heroic effort to rescue children in moral danger is told in Elisabeth Elliot's book *A Chance to Die*. The church today needs to be jolted awake to realize our children are in moral danger. Our efforts should be no less heroic than Amy Carmichael's.

> Dates had particular significance for Amy Carmichael. . . .
> Like the Israelites who, at the command of God, set up piles
> of stones to remind them of places where God had met them
> in a particular way, Amy established certain days to remind
> the Family of His providences. Because Preena arrived on the

sixth of March (1901), and Indraneela died on the sixth of
January (1905), a day of prayer was instituted on the sixth day
of every month to intercede for children in danger. It is still
kept. The Family gathers and kneels, one of the members
reads out the names of villages, and the whole group
responds, "Lord, save the children there." Amy made a Praise
Box into which slips of paper giving reasons for thanksgiving
were dropped. This was opened on the Day of Prayer, and the
Family gave thanks together.[5]

Amy wrote the following about the principles on which
Dohnavur was founded:

It matters that we should be true to one another, be loyal to
what is a family—only a little family in the great Household,
but still a family, with family love alive in it and acting as a living bond . . . prayer is the core of our day. Take prayer out, and
the day would collapse, would be pithless, a straw blown in
the wind. But how can you pray—really pray, I mean—with
one against whom you have a grudge or whom you have been
discussing critically with another? Try it. You will find it cannot be done.[6]

Christ's Crown and Covenant bring cohesion and coherence to
family and church life. His Crown and Covenant will give us a sin-
gleness of heart to pray for our children as Amy prayed for the children of India.

> *Father, hear us, we are praying,*
> *Hear the words our hearts are saying,*
> *We are praying for our children.*
>
> *Keep them from the powers of evil,*
> *From the secret, hidden peril,*
> *From the whirlpool that would suck them,*
> *From the treacherous quicksand pluck them.*

*From the worldling's hollow gladness,*
*From the sting of faithless sadness,*
*Holy Father, save our children.*

*Through life's troubled waters steer them,*
*Through life's bitter battle cheer them,*
*Father, Father, be Thou near them.*
*Read the language of our longing,*
*Read the wordless pleadings thronging,*
*Holy Father, for our children*
  *And wherever they may bide,*
  *Lead them Home at eventide.*[7]

*Question:* What is the relationship between the home and church?

*Answer:* Family solidarity strengthens the church, and community solidarity strengthens the family. Kingdom values and identity must have priority in family life, and families must have priority in church life. Church and family must be driven by an unswerving commitment to Christ's Crown and Covenant.

## BECOMING A COVENANT-KEEPER

1. Read Isaiah 59:21 and 60:1-5. Record your thoughts about this glorious passage.

2. Read Romans 15:5-7. What is your attitude toward those within your church who may be different from you? Does your desire for a testimony of unity that will glorify God override your differences? Pray that it will be so.

3. Read Psalm 127. Do you view the children in your church as

gifts from the Lord? Pray that God will show you one child or one family that He would have you encourage this week.

4.    Continue to pray Colossians 2:2-3 for your church.

CHRISTIAN EDUCATION IDEA

Grace Baptist Church in Cape Coral, Florida, works to maintain the balance between home and church. They are attentive to the details necessary to maintain a fellowship where parents can immerse their children in the life of the church. The following excerpts from the church brochure declare the value of the family and of children:

> Family: Everyone is talking about "Family Values" today, but no one seems to know what it means. Our esteem of the family grows out of the Bible's teaching that God is Architect of the home. He brings the husband and wife together; He is the Giver of children; He has special regard for the widow and fatherless. In trying to make God's priorities our priorities, we emphasize the importance of a healthy, spiritually growing home life. Our programs and schedule reflect this commitment. We guard against unnecessary meetings in order to provide time for family growth in the home. A vast array of resources, including books, tapes, sermons, and seminars are offered to enhance Christian living in the home.
>
> Children: Children are a high priority with us. . . . We view them as blessings given directly by God (Psalm 127:3). This commitment gives rise to two specific emphases in ministry: First, we strongly encourage parents to develop the very best skills possible for raising their children. Second, we accept the responsibility as a church to assist parents in nurturing and caring for their children. . . .
>
> Fellowship: We genuinely love one another. . . . We are discovering that the grace of God in Christ Jesus transcends all of our differences and individual distinctions so that we can have true unity. We are growing in our understanding of

what the Bible means when it tells us that we are "members one of another" (Rom. 12:5). So we share our lives with one another, encourage each other, "rejoice with those who rejoice, and weep with those who weep" (Rom. 12:15).

The pastor, Tom Ascol, regularly teaches a parenting class, but it is not just for parents. All church members are encouraged to attend. All members make a spoken covenant to accept responsibility for the children. Children and parents know that if a child misbehaves or is disrespectful, it is acceptable in this community for any adult present to lovingly correct the child. If the child resists the verbal correction, the adult takes the child to the parent.

The back two pews in the sanctuary are reserved for parents who are teaching their young children how to conduct themselves in worship services. There are many retired people in the church and they frequently baby-sit for young families. These kinds of provisions create an environment where the entire congregation is involved in living covenantally.

# 5
~

# *A Covenantal Strategy for Church Growth*

$$\sim$$

## LIVING AND TEACHING
## COVENANTALLY

### A LOCAL CHURCH

Our church resembles a healthy, functional family. It is a wonderful representation of a biblical model in all areas, but covenant life is especially evident in the safety that is provided for teens and their families.

We arrived at the church when our son was at the tender age of sixteen. Former experiences where teens were not loved well had battered him. Ryan did not want to go to this new church with us for fear this experience would be like the others. We forced him to go. Ryan was not happy. He wore dirty jeans and shoes with holes in them to this church composed primarily of professional businessmen and homemakers who homeschool their children. We squirmed in our seats but did not say anything. We were just thankful Ryan was there with us.

From the first Sunday morning we entered the church, godly men and women spoke with Ryan. They never seemed to notice his apparel. Several of the men invited him to do things with them. Ryan's male Sunday school teacher treated him with great respect. When Ryan bleached his hair, almost every woman in the church complimented him on his new "do." When Ryan brought a female friend to church, the women surrounded her with love and told her how beautiful she looked. After we had been at the church for three months, Ryan said, "Mom, these people are real Christians. They are not hypocrites." As his respect for the people grew, his attitude and even his dress code changed.

Other families have had the same experience with their teens. This palpable love for teens extends beyond the children of our own members. Our church is a predominantly Caucasian congregation, but when a minority homeless teen whom Marlys had been spiritually mothering moved into our home, the other girls and their families enveloped her with love.

When we hosted a party at our home for our church friends, Ryan brought a group of his friends to the party. One was a pregnant teen. The older women introduced themselves to her and showed great love to her. Later a woman offered to help with prenatal expenses.

A new family at our church learned that their teenage son's girlfriend was pregnant. Men and women of the church rallied around this young couple. The women gave her a wedding shower. Almost everyone in the church attended the wedding. They pledged their prayer support to this young couple. One woman became a spiritual mother and sacrificed time and emotional energy to minister to this young wife. They also supported the young man's wounded family.

Our church is a safe place where parents of teens can openly share their most difficult trials and fears regarding their teens. We can make prayer requests for our son and know that many people pray. We are not made to feel that our trials are the result of some mistakes that we must have made.

Teens hear sound biblical doctrine from the pulpit, and they witness covenantal relationships that transcend age, race, or economic status. This is the covenant community as it should be. This is a great place to be.

—John and Marlys Mulkey,
Flower Mound, Texas

# A Covenantal Strategy
# for Church Growth

~

How do we teach the content of the covenant in the context of the covenant community? Thus far we have seen that it begins with a covenantal perspective of Scripture. It involves a balanced approach to the relationship of the home and church. It also involves a covenantal strategy for church growth.

Jesus gave us our marching order when He said, "You will receive power when the Holy Spirit comes on you; and you will be my witnesses in Jerusalem, and in all Judea and Samaria, and to the ends of the earth" (Acts 1:8).

Most church growth specialists agree that the key to church growth is for church members to invite their friends to church. Often this strategy is communicated by a pastor asking his congregation how many came to the church because a friend/neighbor/coworker invited them. The expected answer is usually given. A majority raise their hands, and we all assume that this is the most plausible strategy for church growth. Bad assumption.

I am not minimizing the importance of church members inviting unchurched friends to church. Reaching the lost with the Gospel is surely part of the Great Commission given to us by our Savior, and it is our privilege and responsibility to obey with zeal. What I am saying is that this should not be the front line of offense in a church-growth strategy.

The biblical model for church growth begins with covenant families. The seed of Christian parents should be our primary target group. The first question that should be asked when communicating a strategy for church growth is: How many adult members have a "Timothy testimony" (2 Timothy 3:15) and have known the holy Scriptures "from infancy"? It is in answer to this question that we should see the most enthusiastic show of hands. It is affirmative answers to this question that will energize the church for the second wave of church gro· vth, the unchurched.

Children of Christian parents are leaving the church. They are being sucked up by the messages, activities, and relationships of the world. No matter how many new converts we bring in the front door of the church, if we lose our children out the back door, we are missing the starting point of the Great Commission. We are to begin in Jerusalem. We are to begin where we are. We are to begin in our own homes and with the children in our own churches. If we don't, why should Judea, Samaria, and the ends of the earth give any credence to our message? Why should they want what we have if it is not potent enough to hold on to our own children?

We are not losing our children because the world has more to offer. The world holds out a lie. We have truth. The world cannot deliver on its promises. Our God is a promise-keeper. Perhaps one reason we are losing our children is the lack of emphasis we put on the educational ministry of the church.

## CHRISTIAN EDUCATION—A KEY TO CHURCH GROWTH

Obviously a strong Christian education program is not the only church-growth strategy that should be employed. But without a substantive Christian education ministry, the other components will fizzle. A Christian education program can support, sustain, and supply all other ministries in the church.

A covenantal approach to discipleship, or Christian education, combines biblical truth and compelling relationships that will help fortify our covenant children against the onslaught of an anti-Christian culture. A covenantal approach to Christian education puts a high premium on our responsibility to nurture our covenant children to be mighty men and women of faith who are trained to confront and conquer their culture for King Jesus.

An energetic focus on nurturing covenant children and covenant families will expand, not negate, going to Judea, Samaria, and the ends of the earth (Acts 1:8). Our sons and daughters will be stalwart testimonies of the power and reality of the Gospel, thus increasing our missionary force as they themselves witness on the playground, at the museum, and on the ball team. My friend Ann Llewelyn's four-year-old grandson found his opportunity at the grocery store.

Zachary is a charmer. He is also a covenant child whose parents are teaching him the covenant way of life. He is learning that his faith is to be integrated into every aspect of life, including his choice of toys. As Zach and his mom cruised the grocery aisles, a woman they passed smiled and talked with him. On the second or third pass-by, the woman said, "Look, little boy, they have_____," and she named the current toy craze. Zach turned on his irresistible charm and said, "Oh, we don't play with_____. That doesn't glorify God." His mom smiled as she continued cruising the grocery aisles, grateful that her child is developing a comprehensive biblical world and life view that equips him to give witness to his faith.

## MOSES' METHOD

Just before the death of Moses and the entrance of the Israelites into the promised land, Moses spoke to the people. You can feel his zeal for these people to continue and flourish as a community of faith. He cast an ambitious vision before them. He gave them a mission, and it was an impossible mission apart from the presence and promise of God. His impassioned speech presented a kingdom-growth strategy. He began by recounting their covenant history and repeatedly reminding them of God's affection for them. His exhortation to live covenantally pulsated with instructions about teaching covenant children the covenant way of life. Kingdom expansion must begin with their children.

But laced throughout his farewell address to these people was his primary passion—Yahweh! Surely Moses wanted them to know that Yahweh must be their passion if they were going to claim their children and conquer the culture for His glory. Over and over and over he pointed them to the Lord. Moses knew that no moral code would empower these people and their children to live in God's presence. It was God's presence that would empower them to practice biblical morality, because as they lived in God's presence, their character would be transformed to reflect His character.

These few excerpts from Deuteronomy 4 through 7 give a taste of the *corporate, generational, and comprehensive* characteristics of the covenant that should characterize the church-growth strategy of the church today. Moses' method was to *confront* them with Yahweh and His covenant promise, *challenge* them to radical obedience in all areas of life, and *caution* them to teach the children carefully *why* they did *what* they did. His words are applicable to us as we seek to claim our children and take possession of our culture for Christ's Crown and Covenant.

Moses taught that covenantal obedience validates our identity to the world.

> *Hear now, O Israel, the decrees and laws I am about to teach you. Follow them so that you may live and may go in and take possession of the land that the LORD, the God of your fathers, is giving you. . . . See, I have taught you decrees and laws as the LORD my God commanded me, so that you may follow them in the land you are entering to take possession of it. Observe them carefully, for this will show your wisdom and understanding to the nations, who will hear about all these decrees and say, "Surely this great nation is a wise and understanding people."*

Moses taught that covenantal privileges and responsibilities are to be taught to the children. Kingdom expansion is not short-sighted. There must be a generational perspective so the next generation will continue to expand the kingdom.

> *What other nation is so great as to have their gods near them the way the LORD our God is near us whenever we pray to*

*him? And what other nation is so great as to have such righ-
teous decrees and laws as this body of laws I am setting before
you today? Only be careful, and watch yourselves closely so
that you do not forget the things your eyes have seen or let
them slip from your heart as long as you live. Teach them to
your children and to their children after them.*

*Remember the day you stood before the LORD your God at
Horeb, when he said to me, "Assemble the people before me to
hear my words so that they may learn to revere me as long as
they live in the land and may teach them to their children."*

*These are the commands, decrees and laws the LORD your
God directed me to teach you to observe in the land that you
are crossing the Jordan to possess, so that you, your children
and their children after them may fear the LORD your God as
long as you live by keeping all his decrees and commands that
I give you, and so that you may enjoy long life.*

*Hear, O Israel: The LORD our God, the LORD is one. Love
the LORD your God with all your heart and with all your soul
and with all your strength. These commandments that I give
you today are to be upon your hearts. Impress them on your
children. Talk about them when you sit at home and when you
walk along the road, when you lie down and when you get up.
Tie them as symbols on your hands and bind them on your
foreheads. Write them on the doorframes of your houses and
on your gates.*

*In the future, when your son asks you, "What is the mean-
ing of the stipulations, decrees and laws the LORD our God
has commanded you?" tell him: "We were slaves of Pharaoh
in Egypt, but the LORD brought us out of Egypt with a
mighty hand. Before our eyes the LORD sent miraculous
signs and wonders—great and terrible—upon Egypt and
Pharaoh and his whole household. But he brought us out from
there to bring us in and give us the land that he promised on
oath to our forefathers. The LORD commanded us to obey all
these decrees and to fear the LORD our God, so that we might
always prosper and be kept alive, as is the case today. . . ."*

Moses taught them *what* to do when they entered the land. He showed them the comprehensiveness of covenant life.

> *When the LORD your God brings you into the land you are entering to possess and drives out before you many nations . . . nations larger and stronger than you—and when the LORD your God has delivered them over to you and you have defeated them, then you must destroy them totally. Make no treaty with them, and show them no mercy. Do not intermarry with them. Do not give your daughters to their sons or take their daughters for your sons, for they will turn your sons away from following me to serve other gods, and the LORD's anger will burn against you and will quickly destroy you. This is what you are to do to them: Break down their altars, smash their sacred stones, cut down their Asherah poles and burn their idols in the fire.*

Moses taught them *why* they were to live covenantally.

> *For you are a people holy to the LORD your God. The LORD your God has chosen you out of all the peoples on the face of the earth to be his people, his treasured possession.*

Moses knew that the thrill of kingdom expansion would fade unless the people remembered how much the King loved them.

> *The LORD did not set his affection on you and choose you because you were more numerous than other peoples, for you were the fewest of all peoples. But it was because the LORD loved you and kept the oath he swore to your forefathers that he brought you out with a mighty hand and redeemed you from the land of slavery, from the power of Pharaoh king of Egypt.*

Moses taught that ultimately kingdom expansion depended on the faithfulness of the King.

*Know therefore that the LORD your God is God; he is the faithful God, keeping his covenant of love to a thousand generations of those who love him and keep his commands.*

Moses' method for kingdom expansion should be emulated by the church today. Moses' method confronts us with the comprehensive character of the covenant. Our covenant relationship with God is to be the unifying principle of life. Our faith is to be integrated into all of life. No thing and no time is outside the scope of this all-encompassing reality. Life is not to be compartmentalized. All of life is to be lived in the presence and for the glory of Yahweh. God's Word is to govern our thinking and living. Our view of the world is determined by God's Word.

Moses' method confronts us with the corporate and generational character of the covenant. The covenant way of life is to be taught in the context of the covenant relationships of the covenant community. The covenant community (the Christian family and church) is to be a flesh-and-blood validation of the covenant message. We are to teach the children who God is, who we are in the kingdom of God because of His covenant with us, how we live covenantally in His presence, and how we live covenantally with one another.

This means that we are all teachers and that we are always teaching—as we expectantly sit in our pews preparing to worship the Lord of Glory or as we write a grocery list instead of participating in worship . . . as we talk with a teen after church about an upcoming test and commit to pray or as we walk by the teens and ignore their presence . . . as we purposefully sit with a group of children at a fellowship dinner and really get to know them or as we always sit with our peers . . . as we gratefully volunteer to keep the nursery so we can rock the covenant babies, or when we say our children are grown and we have done our time . . . as we teach a group of sixth graders about covenant relationships and then take them to visit an elderly shut-in and hear marvelous stories of faith, or as we hurriedly glance through the curriculum on the way to church and are satisfied to get through another lesson. We teach when we rejoice with those who rejoice and when we mourn with those who mourn, when our faith determines how we work and play, how we marry and parent, how we live and how we die.

Moses' method will supply the church of Jesus Christ "a thousand generations of those who love him and keep his commands." Moses' church-growth strategy will equip the church to have a substantive presence in culture that will cause onlookers to say in amazement, "Surely this great nation is a wise and understanding people . . . what other nation is so great as to have such righteous decrees and laws as this body of laws. . . ." This positions us to have an aggressive kingdom expansion strategy that goes into Judea, Samaria, and the ends of the earth.

COVENANT SUCCESSION

In a remarkable paper on the doctrines of "covenant children, covenant nurture, and covenant succession," Pastor Robert S. Rayburn wrote:

> I recently attended a church growth seminar . . . . Listed as topics for possible consideration were more than a dozen subjects bearing on ways and means to enlarge the church. Conspicuous by its absence was any mention of anything having to do with the birth and subsequent nurture of the church's children, even though it is easy to prove that since the church's beginning in Eden and still today the primary instrument of her growth has been that of covenant succession. . . .
>
> The remarkable phenomenon of succession of Christian faith through generations, fundamental as it is to the life of the church in the world, is provided a comprehensive explanation in Holy Scripture. It is neither an actual coincidence that the largest number of Christians have Christian parents, nor is it simply a phenomenon left unaccounted for. Everywhere in

the Bible the Lord declares it to be his purpose that Christian marriages produce a holy seed (Mal. 2:15). One of the primary features of the covenant the Lord established with his people is that it embraces families and has always in view the continuation of its saving blessing for generations to come. The place this feature occupies in the divine economy of salvation is indicated by its comprehensive and emphatic reiteration throughout Scripture (e.g., Exod. 20:6; Deut. 4:37-40; Ps. 100:5; 102:28; 103:17-18; Isa. 44:3; 54:13; 59:21; 65:23; Jer. 32:38-39; 35:19; Ezek. 37:25; Zec. 10:6-7; Acts 2:38-39; 16:14-15, 31). It must be plainly stated that the promise made to the children of the covenant is not that of a special status of privilege but is precisely the promise of the gospel, eternal life in heaven. Whether the form of the promise is that God should be their God (Gen. 17:7), or that he will extend to them his righteousness (Ps. 103:17), or his Spirit (Isa. 59:21), or his forgiveness (Acts 2:38-39), or his salvation (Acts 16:31), the covenant which thus embraces the children with their believing parents is the covenant of *grace*.

That the Lord should so direct his saving love down the lines of generations is only to be expected of a Father who knows what it is to love a son and to suffer a son to fall under the divine wrath and who teaches his own children that "everyone who loves the father loves his child as well" (1 John 5:1). It is only to love his people genuinely and deeply that the Father should also love their children, whom John Flavel, with a parent's insight, somewhere describes as "pieces of themselves wrapped in another skin." Imagine the contrary: that Christian parents brought children into the world with no confidence at all that the saving grace which had been pitched upon them—among the comparatively few in all the world so favored—would likewise be pitched upon their children, whom they love as they love life itself. Christian parents do not imagine themselves to be populating hell when they bring sons and daughters into the world! Their hope and expectation are otherwise (Ps. 90:16). . . . It is a true Father and a perfect fatherly love that made and then so often repeated the promise to be God to his people *and to their children.*

The biblical paradigm is for covenant children to grow up in faith from infancy. . . .

It is imperative that the doctrine of covenant succession be recovered in our churches. Its loss has deeply diminished the church's appreciation of and wonder over the liberality and perfection of divine grace. Further, the appropriation by faith of this divine promise and summons is the means appointed to furnish the church with generation after generation of great multitudes of Christian servants and soldiers who reach manhood and womanhood well taught, sturdy in faith, animated by love for God and man, sophisticated in the ways of the world and the Devil, polished in the manners of genuine Christian brotherhood, overshadowed by the specter of the Last Day, nerved to deny themselves and take up their cross so as to be counted worthy of greater exploits for Christ and Kingdom. Presently the church not only suffers a terrible shortage of such other-worldly and resolute Christians, superbly prepared for spiritual warfare, but, in fact, is hemorrhaging its children into the world. Christian evangelism will never make a decisive difference in our culture when it amounts merely to an effort to replace losses due to widespread desertion from our own camp. The gospel will always fail to command attention and carry conviction when large numbers of those who grow up under its influence are observed abandoning it for the world . . . inscribing the doctrine of covenant succession upon the heart of family and church must have a wonderfully solemnizing and galvanizing effect. It will set Christian parents seriously to work on the spiritual nurture of their children, equipping them and requiring them to live the life of covenant faith and duty to which their God and Savior called them at the headwaters of life. And, ever conscious of the greater effect of parental example, they will forsake the easy way, shamelessly and joyfully to live a life of devotion and obedience which adorns and enables the faith in the eyes of their children. This they will do, who embrace the Bible's doctrine, lest the Lord on the Great Day should say to them: "You took your sons and daughters whom you bore to me and sacrificed them to idols."[1]

## COVENANT CHILDREN

Dr. Rayburn's paper is remarkable, and the testimony of his own family is a confirmation of the paper. His father was the founder of Covenant Seminary and Covenant College. There are many stories of the faithfulness of this family of unwavering warriors for Christ's Crown and Covenant. One of the most recent examples was the death of his forty-nine-year-old sister Bronwyn after a thirty-two-month battle with cancer. Her husband, Chaplain Steve Leonard, tells the story in a letter to Covenant College alumni:

> Bronwyn was a valiant covenant saint to the very threshold of heaven when she gloriously passed from our presence, giving us a glimpse of her greeting there. She "crossed the river" on Sunday night, the "day of all the days the best." Throughout her whole life, she loved the Lord's Day and so entered into eternal rest on that day of rest.
>
> It was so like *Pilgrim's Progress*—for Bronwyn, suffocating for air as fluids filled her lungs, crossed the river and "stepped on the far shore." As Linnea (her daughter) expressed how much we would miss her, but that she would in minutes be with the Lord Jesus and Papa (Dad R.) and Moses, Abraham, et. al ... Bronwyn got a joyful and childlike look on her face— opened her eyes wide—and speaking without gasping for air for a number of minutes, nonstop she spoke of Paul, Mark, Joshua, and Caleb (not her sons who bear those names), and Dad—and though so overwhelmed at the large greeting said a number of times, "Everybody is here." And "Hallelujah." When Linnea said, "Mummy, you won't be gone from us long; we are going to follow you soon," Bronwyn said so

clearly and firmly, "Hurry!" So we must. Hurry to Christ. Hurry to the Word. Hurry to prayer. Hurry to believe and obey. Hurry to heaven.

## A COVENANTAL LEGACY

One of the most captivating stories I have ever heard is the rich legacy of faith left by Ann Hamilton. She lived from approximately 1750 to 1800.

According to Bill Armes, a seventh-generation descendant, she was known in her Scottish village as a devout Christian whose countenance radiated the peace of her Lord. The story has been handed down from generation to generation that on her deathbed, her family observed that her sweet countenance changed to one of worry and anxiety. They asked what was wrong. She was finally able to give them an answer, and when she did, her expression changed once more to radiance. "Children," she said, "I have it. He has given me the promise." And she quoted Isaiah 59:21: "'As for me, this is my covenant with them, saith the Lord; My Spirit that is upon thee, and my words which I have put in thy mouth, shall not depart out of thy mouth, nor out of the mouth of thy seed, nor out of the mouth of thy seed's seed, saith the Lord, from henceforth and for ever'" (KJV).

She was claiming that covenant promise for the future, and God has honored His promise to that Scottish mother.

Among her fifth-generation descendants are John Armes, Willard Armes, Katherine Armes Holliday, and Janet Armes Ludlam. The men are Presbyterian ministers, and the women are wives of ministers. All of their children are committed Christians—some serving as pastors, missionaries, heads of Christian schools, deacons, elders, chaplains. One had strayed from the faith, only to be convicted upon hearing of Ann Hamilton's story. Today he is in the ministry.

The story has been shared at family baptisms and funerals. The covenant verse was engraved on a silver plaque many years ago that was passed on to Willard, and duplicates now hang in the homes of most living descendants. Whenever and however it is told or read, it is a powerful testimony of God's covenant promises.

There are now sixty-one grandchildren who are hearing the story from their parents, continuing the covenantal chain claimed by Ann Hamilton so many years ago.[2]

Ann Hamilton had a covenantal church-growth strategy. She believed God's covenant promise, and she claimed future generations for King Jesus.

HOVERING MERCY

Stories such as the ones above are celebrations of God's covenant faithfulness to families, but they are painful for Christian parents whose children are indifferent or rebellious toward God. No matter how bent a child is on self-destruction, Christian parents must tenaciously hold on to God's promises and continue in prayer for that wayward child. Monica, the mother of Augustine, prayed for thirty-two years for her son's conversion. His licentious lifestyle broke her heart, but not her confidence in God. God answered her prayer and used her son to change the course of history.

In his *Confessions*, "one of the most moving diaries ever recorded of a man's journey to the fountain of God's grace,"[3] Augustine wrote of his pre-conversion years, "To Carthage I came, where they sang all around me in my ears a cauldron of unholy loves. . . . my soul was sickly and full of sores, it miserably cast itself forth, desiring to be scraped by the touch of objects of sense. . . ."[4] Yet he writes of this time, "Thy faithful mercy hovered over me afar."[5]

Of his mother he wrote:

And Thou sentest Thine hand from above, and drewest my soul out of that profound darkness, my mother, Thy faithful one, weeping to Thee for me, more than mothers weep the bodily deaths of their children. For she, by that faith and spirit which she had from Thee, discerned the death wherein I lay, and Thou heardest her, O Lord; Thou heardest her, and despisedst not her tears, when streaming down, they watered the ground under her eyes in every place where she prayed; yea Thou heardest her.[6]

He writes that Monica was encouraged by a bishop who said to her, "Go thy way, and God bless thee, for it is not possible that the son of these tears should perish."[7]

And Augustine praises God for His grace and for Monica's prayers: "For Thy hands, O my God, in the secret purpose of Thy providence, did not forsake my soul; and out of my mother's heart's blood, through her tears night and day poured out, was a sacrifice offered for me unto Thee; and Thou didst deal with me by wondrous ways."[8]

It has been said that Augustine of Hippo influenced Christian thinking more than any other church father. And behind it all, from our vantage point, we see a covenantal church-growth strategy—the persevering prayers of his mother and the persevering grace of God.

## CHURCH GROWTH . . . CHRISTIAN EDUCATION

A covenantal church-growth strategy will be so intertwined with the Christian education program that they will at times be indistinguishable. Each will strengthen and fuel the other.

I am convinced that when God's people begin to see Jesus on every page of Scripture and on every page of our lives, when we understand the connection between faith and life, when we comprehend the reality of living all of life in God's presence, our hearts will burn with a consuming passion to embrace our privileges as citizens of the kingdom and our glorious responsibility to pass kingdom values to the next generation.

Then the educational ministry of the church moves beyond trying to find warm bodies to teach the two-year-olds or naive newcomers to endure the teens, to energized covenant people traditioning covenant life to the next generation.

Then the first line of our church-growth strategy is a strong educational ministry that believes it is just as "spiritual" to teach the first graders as it is to serve on the missions committee or the evangelism committee.

Then those outside the church will see something authentic and compelling. They will see God's covenant people continuing "to meet together in the temple courts. They broke bread in their homes and ate together with glad and sincere hearts, praising God and enjoying the favor of all the people." And we will find the Lord adding "to their number daily those who were being saved" (Acts 2:46-47).

### TAKE-AWAY POINT

A covenantal church-growth strategy works from the inside out. This strategy begins with a conviction that we as a covenant community are commanded to teach the faith to all of the children God gives to our church. This conviction translates into a substantive Christian education ministry. The allocation of energy and resources reflects the high priority we give to the educational ministry of the church. We think strategically about the nurture of our covenant children. We teach them a covenantal perspective of Scripture, and we enfold them into the life of the covenant community. We show our children Jesus on every page of Scripture and on every page of our lives. We are faithful stewards of these gifts entrusted to us by God. We wage war for their souls on the battlefield of prayer.

> O Almighty God, our Heavenly Father, give us such a seed! Give us a seed right with Thee! Smite us and our house with everlasting barrenness rather than that our seed should not be right with Thee. O God, give us our children. Give us our children. A second time, and by a far better birth, give us our children to be beside us in Thy holy covenant. For it had been better we had never been born; it had been better we had never been betrothed; it had been better we had sat all our days solitary unless our children are to be right with Thee. . . .

But Thou, O God, art Thyself a Father, and thus hast in Thyself a Father's heart. Hear us, then, for our children, O our Father. . . . In season and out of season; we shall not go up into our bed; we shall not give sleep to our eyes nor slumber to our eyelids till we and all our seed are right with Thee. And then how we and all our saved seed beside us shall praise Thee . . . and shall say: Unto Him who loved us and washed us from our sins in His own blood, and hath bestowed upon us a free, full, and everlasting forgiveness, and hath made us partakers of His Divine Nature, to Him be our love and praise and service to all eternity. Amen and Amen![9]

*Question:* What is a covenantal strategy for church growth?

*Answer:* A covenantal church-growth strategy begins with the education of covenant children. It is a recognition that our children are gifts from the Lord, and it is an energetic attempt to be good stewards of those gifts. This strategy then moves forward to claim all the world for Christ's Crown and Covenant.

BECOMING A COVENANT-KEEPER

1. Read Deuteronomy 4 through 7 and make a list of the comprehensive characteristics of the covenant. What areas of life are included in these instructions?

2. Read Deuteronomy 4 through 7 and make a list of the corporate characteristics of the covenant. What is said about our responsibilities and privileges as a community?

3. Read Deuteronomy 4 through 7 and make a list of the generational characteristics of the covenant. What emphasis is put on traditioning covenant life to the children?

CHRISTIAN EDUCATION IDEA

We have said much about teaching the content of the covenant in the context of the covenant community. Here are some practical ideas for building community. Most of these ideas are workable for all ages.

Three questions should be asked about every activity, project, and event. Teachers should also consider these questions as they make application of their lessons.

1. How does this build community in our class?
2. How does it build community with other members of our church?
3. How does it advance God's kingdom in the world?

There should be a leadership team with specific people responsible for building community in the class, building community with other groups within the church, and advancing God's kingdom beyond the church.

## Some Ways to Build Community in a Class

1. Have a specific person or committee to coordinate the following: follow-up with visitors, contacting members who have missed two Sundays, planning outings, a prayer chain, compassion ministry to members who are sick or have other special needs.

2. Have greeters so that people feel welcome from the moment they arrive.

3. Put duplicate numbers in a basket and have each person/couple draw a number. Then have people find the other person/couple with the corresponding number. The pairs are to pray for each other for a specified time. Give them time to share prayer requests. Encourage them to do something to encourage the prayer partner(s), such as send a note, have them over for

dinner, bring a batch of cookies, etc. Each week ask if anyone was encouraged by the prayer partner. As others hear, they will be encouraged to do similar things.

4. Allow time for discussing the application of the lesson. If the class is larger than ten, divide into groups of five or six. Many people will discuss in a small group who would never speak out in a large group. Have a life situation or a specific question for the class to discuss to apply the lesson.

5. Occasionally begin the lesson by dividing into small groups and asking all to tell one thing they are thankful for, or one thing the Lord has been teaching them recently, or to share a favorite Scripture verse or hymn. This activity can be done in three to five minutes, but it helps people to get to know one another on a deeper level.

6. Periodically have a fellowship day rather than a lesson.

7. Frequently have a class member give a testimony. This can be a salvation testimony or a testimony about a specific experience. Give very clear written instructions for testimonies. Allow three minutes. Ask people to write the testimony out and time it, and then to stick to their written notes. This does not take significant time from the lesson but will add a wonderful dimension to the unity of the class.

## Building Community with Other Church Groups

1. Each week have everyone sign a card to send to someone in the church. It can be a card of appreciation or encouragement or a get-well card. Have someone pray for the person who will receive the card. This works for all ages. The card can be on a table for people to sign when they enter the room.

2. Occasionally invite a church officer or the chairman of a committee to speak to the class for three minutes and share his/her

ministry burden. The person should tell how the class can pray for that particular ministry. Following the testimony, have a member of the class pray for the person. This is even good for small children. They need to know the leaders of the church and to feel a responsibility to pray for them.

3.  Plan joint parties and ministry projects with a different age group. For example, a senior saints and a first-grade class could visit a nursing home, sing hymns for the residents, and then go out for pizza.

*Ways to Advance God's Kingdom Beyond the Church*

1.  "Adopt" a missionary family. Pray for them and write to them.

2.  Support a specific community project. For example, bring food for a homeless shelter, baby items for a crisis pregnancy center, needed items for an inner-city ministry, cards to shut-ins. Pray regularly for that ministry and occasionally have someone from the ministry come in and speak to the class. If possible, plan projects where class members actually go to the ministry and work.

3.  Participate in Prison Fellowship's Angel Tree project at Christmas.

4.  Contact Joni and Friends for ideas on ministering to families with special-needs children.

# 6

## Teaching Covenantally

~

## LIVING AND TEACHING
## COVENANTALLY

### A CHRISTIAN EDUCATOR

In the midst of preparing for college, I have spent many hours reflecting over the people who have impacted my life. One person in particular comes to mind—my teacher and mentor Dr. George Grant—who continues to have an enormous influence on my view of education. I say "view of education," because G. K. Chesterton said, "The most important fact about the subject of education is that there is no such thing. Education is not a subject and does not deal in subjects. It is instead a transfer of a way of life."

This view of education has shaped my view of learning and applying the Bible to my life. Since learning is a "transfer of a way of life," the goal is to seek understanding continuously. Learning is a means to give direction to an end. An educated person is not the end result, but the end is a person who learns to love God with the mind, as well as with the heart and soul. After sitting under this style of teaching, I am now able to analyze and evaluate new information and knowledge through biblical lenses. In 2 Corinthians 10:5 Paul writes that we are to bring "every thought into captivity to the obedience of Christ." Learning is a means of loving God with our minds.

Dr. Grant's philosophy of education is a biblical classical model he has implemented at Franklin Classical School, a parent-directed school in Franklin, Tennessee. He taught me that this "transfer of a way of life" is attainable only by the method of mentor to a disciple. The difference between a mentor and a teacher is that a mentor seeks to invest himself in a relationship with the disciple. A mentor encourages and challenges the disciple spiritually and intellectually, while a teacher may only impart information. Dr. Grant gives testimony to God's ever-transforming grace by equipping the next generation of leaders—a vision driven by faith. Hebrews 11:1 says, "Now faith is the substance of things hoped for, the evidence of things not seen." The mentor accepts that he may not see all of the results of his investment, but he does not lose hope.

G. K. Chesterton also said, "Remember: if anything is worth doing, then it is worth doing badly," meaning, that when something is worth doing, it is just worth doing. This is the outworking of the faith that has driven Dr. Grant to be a mentor to so many— not a rejection of excellence, but a motivation to begin obedience instead of waiting for perfect circumstances. This way of thinking gave me the desire and the confidence to teach a Bible study at Franklin Classical School during my junior and senior years of high school.

Dr. Grant's passion for learning and vision for discipleship has immensely affected my world and life view. At graduation he exhorted the senior class as the next generation of leaders with these words, "You have a destiny, and the time is now to act upon it! May God help you be what you have been called to be, and do what you have been called to do. God bless you."

By the work of the Holy Spirit, I am able to respond to the truth of the Gospel, which is written on my heart. May God teach me to serve His kingdom by obeying His Word. May He use me to disciple others as I have been discipled.

—Elizabeth Taylor
Brentwood, Tennessee

# *Teaching Covenantally*

$\approx$

Most current educational methods and content focus on helping students feel good about themselves. It seems that it does not matter if we are raising a generation of illiterates as long as they have positive self-images. It is sad that many well-meaning churches have embraced this trend. The decline in solid Christian education that exalts our Savior has resulted in an increased interest in our significance. This in turn has given birth to a therapeutic theology that focuses on our needs rather than on God's glory. And the interesting thing is that we have not become stronger Christians. In fact, in some churches the offices once occupied by Christian educators have been turned over to counselors who are often dealing with the fallout of our lack of Christian education.

It is time to return to a vigorous emphasis on a covenantal approach to Christian education.

A biblical approach to teaching never trivializes the educational process nor incapacitates the students with self-centered nonsense. There is far too much at stake. There is knowledge to be acquired and applied that has eternal ramifications. There is a glorious God to be glorified. There is a kingdom to be advanced. Psalm 78 is a Christian education psalm that gives us a foundation on which to build a Christian education ministry.

As you read this chapter, don't miss the richness of Psalm 78 by limiting it to small children and to formal teaching situations. Remember that all believers are covenant children and that we are all Christian educators. This psalm is about the covenant community in action.

THE RESPONSIBILITY

*O my people, hear my teaching; listen to the words of my mouth. I will open my mouth in parables, I will utter hidden things, things from of old—what we have heard and known, what our fathers have told us. We will not hide them from their children; we will tell the next generation the praiseworthy deeds of the LORD, his power, and the wonders he has done.*

—*Psalm 78:1-4*

Whose responsibility is it to teach the children? Most evangelicals quickly answer that it is the responsibility of the father as the head of the home. As we saw in chapter 3, that is partially right.

Psalm 78 is spoken to the covenant community: *"O my people."* The command to *"tell the next generation"* is given to individual fathers in a community context. Educating covenant children is a family affair and a community affair. It does take a village to raise a child. It takes a village of faith, the church of the Lord Jesus, to reinforce, expand, model, and practice what is being taught in the home.

We will consider three implications of this principle.

First, it is the responsibility of parents to instruct their children at home and to have their families participate in the covenant community of faith. Children are to see their parents celebrating the privilege of being a member of Christ's body and assuming responsibilities to help care for the body. Moms and dads who rejoice with those who rejoice and mourn with those who mourn (Romans 12:15), who are kind, compassionate, and forgiving to others (Ephesians 4:32), who consider how they can spur others on to love and good deeds (Hebrews 10:24), who pray for others (James 5:16), and who offer hospitality without grumbling (1 Peter 4:9), teach their children that this is the way God's people live in covenant with one another.

Second, those who are in formal teaching positions in the children's ministry of the church must understand that they cannot teach a child covenantally without knowing that child's parents. There must be communication and cooperation between the home and the church. The wise teacher will deliberately and intentionally open the way for parental involvement. This can be done with letters to parents telling them what the children will be studying and offering suggestions as to how the parents can reinforce the lessons, by inviting a different parent each week to assist in the class, by asking parents to plan service projects and outings for the children, and by making periodic home visits or telephone calls.

Cheryl teaches a Sunday school class of five-year-olds. Each August when she receives the list of children who will be promoted to her class in September, she writes the following letter to the parents.

Dear Parents:

I am excited that _____ will be in my class this year. Teaching God's Word to children is a precious privilege and an enormous responsibility. No one knows or loves your child like you do. In order to make the most of the opportunity God is giving me to teach your child, I need your help.

First, please pray for me.

Second, please accompany your child to our class on (date) and plan to stay with us for the first fifteen minutes so that I can get to know you and so I can tell you some of the things we will be doing in Sunday school.

Third, fill out the enclosed form and return it to me when you bring your child on (date).

My prayer for our class is that the children will "grow in the grace and knowledge of our Lord and Savior Jesus Christ" (2 Peter 3:18) and that we will be "encouraged in heart and united in love, so that they may have the full riches of complete understanding, in order that they may know the mystery of God, namely, Christ, in whom are hidden all the treasures of wisdom and knowledge" (Colossians 2:2-3). Please join me in this prayer.

For God's Glory,

Cheryl

In the form that accompanies the letter, Cheryl asks for general information such as the child's birthday. She asks if there are any learning problems or styles or any situations that she should know about in order to minister to the child. She asks the parents to prayerfully set a spiritual goal for their child. She explains that knowing their goals will help her to be more focused in her praying and in her teaching. And she gives several options for parents to be involved such as assisting with crafts or music, planning outings or service projects, and being in the class to help welcome children and handle the roll.

There is a treasure chest of stories about the impact of this letter. One year a mother, who was a church member but who did not take her child to Sunday school, appeared on promotion Sunday. She told Cheryl that she never made the effort to get up early enough to attend Sunday school, but she never knew anyone who loved her child enough to write the things Cheryl expressed in her letter. "I want my child in your class," she said. This meant that an entire family became active in Sunday school and moved from the periphery of church life into the mainstream.

Many parents have never considered setting a spiritual goal for their children each year. Their hearts have been knit together in a loving partnership with Cheryl as together they prayed for a character trait to be developed or an attitude to be changed, and as they celebrated God's grace in the child's life as those prayers were answered. Numerous young parents have helped in Cheryl's class and discovered a new passion to teach God's Word to children. Her class is a training ground for many who have asked to help her on a regular basis.

Third, those involved in adult education should be intentional in helping their students build bridges to other age-groups. Adult classes can adopt a class of children or teens. They can assign each member one of the children/teens. The members pray regularly for the young person and write notes of encouragement to him or her. Members can plan outings and ministry projects with the group of young people. The adults can develop helping relationships with single parents of children/teens.

The entire covenant community is enriched when a Christian education program plans ways to help the community assume its covenant responsibilities.

## THE PROCESS

> *He decreed statutes for Jacob and established the law in Israel,*
> *which he commanded our forefathers to teach their children,*
> *so the next generation would know them, even the children*
> *yet to be born, and they in turn would tell their children. Then*
> *they would put their trust in God and would not forget his*
> *deeds but would keep his commands.*
>
> *Psalm 78:5-7*

This passage gives us a glimpse at the learning process in educating God's people to think and act Christianly. Before we examine this process, let me hasten to say that this is not a formula. We all want a money-back guarantee that if we follow the recipe, our kids will be perfect. The point of this discussion is not to give a formula. The point is to see that too often we are satisfied with the first step in the process rather than prayerfully pursuing the biblical goal. This is not about methods. It is about helping students of all ages cultivate a comprehensive Christian worldview that equips them to glorify God in all of life.

In Christian education, the goal is not self-fulfillment or self-actualization. The intended outcome is not a positive self-image. As set forth in Psalm 78, the goal is for the student to trust God and keep His commands. There is a process that parents and churches are to follow to help move students toward that goal.

This learning process is the same in informal and formal teaching situations. It is the same when parents impress God's Word on their children as they "sit at home" and "walk along the road" (Deuteronomy 6:7), when the preschool Sunday school teacher, the youth leader, the day school teacher, and the teacher of adults teach a lesson. The learning process is basically the same each time we learn something new.

First, there are statutes and laws to be *taught*. There is information to be communicated by the parents and church to the students. The statutes and laws are God's Word. Paul said to the Ephesian elders that he was "innocent of the blood of all men" (Acts 20:26). Then he gives the reason that he could make such a claim: "For I have not hesitated to proclaim to you the whole will of God" (Acts 20:27).

Second, once the data is in the brain, the teacher is to challenge the student to process it prayerfully until it moves to the heart. The student must *know* the information in such a way that it makes a difference in how and what he thinks.

Third, the learning process is not complete until the student *puts his trust in God and keeps His commands*. The statutes and laws are to be the "rule for faith and life."[1] The information is to shape the student's view of the world and of his life and is to be his authority for how he lives.

Our grandchildren memorize Scripture from the time they can talk. One of our family favorites is Proverbs 3:5-6: "Trust in the LORD with all your heart and lean not on your own understanding; in all your ways acknowledge him, and he will make your paths straight."

Four-year-old Daniel says this verse with much enthusiasm, but he cannot tell you what it means to *trust* or to *acknowledge*. However, eight-year-old Hunter has moved to the early stage of the second level. He can talk about the verse and give some verbal explanation of what it means. He understands this verse in the context of believing that Jesus died for his sins, and he is beginning to understand that he is to acknowledge God's authority in all decisions. Sometimes he even moves to the third stage and applies it to a given situation.

The adult members of our family frequently realize that though we have recited this verse for years, we continually move to a deeper and richer understanding of its meaning and application. One of the marvelous things about learning God's Word is that it is cyclical in the sense that when we go full circle and obey it, we start back over and advance to a greater understanding and application.

Perhaps you have already noticed the similarity between this three-stage process and the trivium of classical education (grammar, logic, and rhetoric). Classical education is not a formula. It is not a method. It is a way of thinking and living. It is faith and life. Classical Christian education is the development of a comprehensive biblical worldview and a life of obedience.

George Grant explains that classical education

> . . . equipped generations of students with the tools for a lifetime of learning: a working knowledge of the timetables of history, a background understanding of the great literary classics, a structural competency in Greek and Latin-based grammars, a familiarity with the sweep of art, music, and ideas, a grasp of research and writing skills, a worldview comprehension for math and science basics, a principle approach to current events, and an emphasis on a Christian life paradigm. . . . Very simply, it is a conscious return to those academic disciplines and methodologies—the very notions that helped to spark the great cultural flowering of Western Christendom over the past thousand years—emphasizing the basic thinking and character skills necessary to launch young men and women on a lifetime journey of growth and learning. It is an approach that involves a good deal of hard work—as does anything worthwhile—but it is not a system of education for the intellectuals only. Rather classical education is a simple affirmation that all of us need to be grounded in the good things, the great things, the true things.[2]

As we dissect this process and analyze each part, keep in mind that this has application to the Christian day school/home school as well as the church's Sunday programs, Bible clubs, youth groups, and home Bible studies. The church's programs, no less than the day school, should be helping to shape a biblical worldview and a life of obedience.

## STAGE ONE: STATUTES AND LAWS

*He decreed statutes for Jacob and established the law in Israel,
which he commanded our forefathers to teach their children. . . .*

In the first stage of this process, the student learns the stories and
characters of the Bible. He memorizes Bible verses and passages.
He learns the "language" of the Bible. At this stage he usually
does not fully understand the language, but gradually meaning
is attached to the words and events. This is true for the infant
growing up in the church and for the adult convert. As one man
who had been a Christian less than a year said, "This is all new to
me. I am hearing new words, hearing about people and events I
never heard of before, and hearing about a totally new way of life.
It is like learning a foreign language. Gradually it is making sense,
but please be patient with me because it is so new." A young
woman who grew up in the church but did not become a
Christian until adulthood said, "I am grateful for my church background. Even though I grew up in a church that was not evangelistic, I did hear about the people and events in the Bible. I learned
the great hymns of the faith. I did develop the practice of attending church. When I became a Christian, it was as if I had a jump-
start in my spiritual growth. Things were familiar and quickly
made sense."

Chucking biblical words, people, and events in order to be
"seeker-friendly" robs our students of the rich heritage of biblical
truth and stifles their growth in grace. A diet devoid of words such
as *justification, sanctification,* and *glorification* stunts their understanding of the wonder of our inheritance as God's children. When
a child is born into our family, we do not revert to cooing and bab-
bling in order to be baby-friendly. Our language does not change.
In fact, I intentionally use words I want the children to learn. It is
fun to hear them use words they have heard from the adults around
them. They do not fully understand what they are saying, but gradually they attach meaning to the words.

The covenant community needs to learn the language of faith. Every member, regardless of age, needs to know the words and stories of redemption. These words and stories need to be taught from a covenantal perspective (see chapter 3). Studies confirm that even those who have grown up in the church are woefully ignorant of the content of the Bible. To encourage application of truth without teaching the content of truth produces a fragile obedience. It is a house built on sand (Matthew 7:24-27). The wise man builds his house on the rock. Wise Christian educators take the time to anchor their students on the solid rock of God's Word.

## STAGE TWO: KNOWING

*. . . so the next generation would know them . . .*

In this stage the student takes the information he has learned and begins to put it into a context. He takes the individual collection of people and events and begins to see the thread that holds them together. He sees them in their flow of redemption history. As they are threaded together, each individual part becomes more potent because the student sees its linkage to the whole. People and events do not exist in isolation. They are part of the grand drama of redemption that is moving toward its ultimate climax. So it is logical that after explaining this process, the psalmist launches into a narration of Israel's history (Psalm 78:9-72).

*The Theological Wordbook of the Old Testament* explains this stage of the process:

Knowledge of God is derived from those outstanding historical events in which God has evidenced and has revealed himself to chosen individuals such as Abraham and Moses. These revelations are to be taught to others. "Knowledge of God" appears in parallel with "fear of the Lord" (Isa 11:2; cf. 58:2; Jer 22:16) as a description of true religion. The man who has a right relation with God confesses him and obeys him.

To do justice and righteousness and to judge the cause of the poor and the needy is to know God (Jer 22:15-16). On the other hand, where there is no knowledge of God, there is swearing, lying, killing, stealing, committing adultery, and breaking all bonds (Hos 4:1-2). Such will bring destruction upon a people (Hos 4:6; cf. Isa 5:13). Knowledge of God is more pleasing to him than sacrifice (Hos 6:6). The prophetic view of the Messianic age is of a time in which the knowledge of God covers the earth as water covers the sea (Hab 2:14; cf. Isa 11:9).[3]

The covenant community needs to know its history. The stories of the heroes and heroines of faith down through the ages give us shoulders to stand on as we face our moment in history. When the writer of Hebrews exhorts us not to "shrink back" (Hebrews 10:39), he fortifies us for the task by reminding us of the faith of Abel, Enoch, Noah, Abraham, and many other saints of old (Hebrews 11). Their stories give us a deeper knowledge of God. We need to tell the stories of Scripture and the stories of saints down through the ages who have lived as faithful pilgrims.

On a trip to Scotland, I discovered an old book entitled *Selections for the Young.* It was published in the mid-nineteenth century by the General Assembly of the Free Church of Scotland. It is a collection of brief stories of Scottish reformers and divines. There is the story of the call of John Knox to the ministry, of dying sayings of eminent Scots, of the martyrdom of early Scottish Protestants. There are hymns, poetry, and quotes. My soul is stirred to greater obedience as I read of these saints who did not shrink back.

But I wonder if such stories are being written in the fabric of church history today. What stories will children read at the end of the twenty-first century about the church at the end of the twentieth century? Even more piercing is the question of what stories my own great-grandchildren will hear about the threads of our family history.

## STAGE THREE: TRUST AND OBEY

*Then they would put their trust in God and would not forget his deeds but would keep his commands.*

In this stage the student acts upon the knowledge he has learned. His trust in God is substantive because it is grounded on a knowledge of who God is and what He has done. This head and heart trust produces obedience.

The wise teacher helps his students build bridges from knowing to doing. He is alert to the life stage and life situations of his students and liberally illustrates how truth applies to that stage and those situations. He is always watching for glimpses of the application of truth into life situations. But the wise teacher is keenly aware that truth must go beyond head knowledge and behavioral change. The wise teacher prays for hearts that are loyal to God.

## A MATTER OF THE HEART

*They would not be like their forefathers—a stubborn and rebellious generation, whose hearts were not loyal to God, whose spirits were not faithful to him.*

*—Psalm 78:8*

The psalmist writes that students are to receive the same information that their fathers received, but the desired outcome is that they will not be like their forefathers who were a stubborn and rebellious generation. The psalmist forcefully confronts us with the reality that hearing the information will not make the decisive difference. It is a change of heart that will produce trust and obedience. The statutes and laws will not save our students. They need a heart transplant. They are sin-prone, and apart from grace they will blindly follow their natural tendencies. The psalmist drives this point home by describing the faithlessness of the people and the faithfulness of God.

*The men of Ephraim, though armed with bows, turned back on the day of battle; they did not keep God's covenant and refused to live by his law.*

*They forgot what he had done, the wonders he had shown them. He did miracles in the sight of their fathers in the land of Egypt, in the region of Zoan. . . .*

*But they continued to sin against him, rebelling in the desert against the Most High. . . .*

*Whenever God slew them, they would seek him; they eagerly turned to him again. They remembered that God was their Rock, that God Most High was their Redeemer.*

*But then they would flatter him with their mouths, lying to him with their tongues; their hearts were not loyal to him, they were not faithful to his covenant.*

*Yet he was merciful; he forgave their iniquities and did not destroy them. Time after time he restrained his anger and did not stir up his full wrath.*

*He remembered that they were but flesh, a passing breeze that does not return.*

*How often they rebelled against him in the desert and grieved him in the wasteland! Again and again they put God to the test; they vexed the Holy One of Israel.*

—Psalm 78:9-41

We and our students vex the Holy One of Israel. We and they are in desperate need of grace. To settle for head knowledge and behavioral change apart from a changed heart is not Christian education. Educating Christianly bores through the brain and goes deep into the inner man. This drives us to cast ourselves and our students on the mercy of God, because "the man without the Spirit does not accept the things that come from the Spirit of God, for they are foolishness to him, and he cannot understand them, because they are spiritually discerned" (1 Corinthians 2:14).

It is not a matter of mental astuteness. The work of the Holy Spirit is absolutely essential, and He is absolutely sovereign. Our students do not have the spiritual ability to move beyond mental comprehension of information to a spiritual understanding of God's Word. God's Spirit will take His Word and accomplish His purpose.

> *So is my word that goes out from my mouth: It will not return to me empty, but will accomplish what I desire and achieve the purpose for which I sent it.*
>
> *—Isaiah 55:11*

> *For the word of God is living and active. Sharper than any double-edged sword, it penetrates even to dividing soul and spirit, joints and marrow; it judges the thoughts and attitudes of the heart.*
>
> *—Hebrews 4:12*

We are now talking about the transforming power of the Gospel. I am not minimizing the importance of thorough preparation, of carefully crafted lessons, and of caring relationships, but this is something no lesson plan or human relationship can accomplish. This is the supernatural work of God's Holy Spirit. We are now on holy ground. This is a wonder that transcends this earthly realm. When we teach God's Word, we participate with His Spirit to accomplish His purpose. Make no mistake, the nonessential in this equation is the teacher. God does not need us, but He graciously chooses to use us.

If God's people even begin to scratch the surface of this phenomenon, there will be more volunteers to teach in the educational ministry of the church than can be utilized. Sunday school superintendents will have waiting lists of people wanting to be involved in this stupendous enterprise. The teacher who understands this will spend much time in the secret place of prayer. This teacher will realize his need and his students' need for grace.

We must pray, realizing that it is God who creates a new heart: "Create in me a pure heart, O God, and renew a steadfast spirit within me. Do not cast me from your presence or take your Holy Spirit from me" (Psalm 51:10-11).

We must pray, realizing that it is God who turns a person's heart toward His Word: "Turn my heart toward your statutes and not toward selfish gain" (Psalm 119:36).

We must pray, realizing that it is God who removes the heart of stone and gives a heart of flesh: "I will give them an undivided heart and put a new spirit in them; I will remove from them their heart of stone and give them a heart of flesh. Then they will follow my decrees and be careful to keep my laws. They will be my people, and I will be their God" (Ezekiel 11:19-20).

And we must pray, realizing that this is spiritual warfare: "For though we live in the world, we do not wage war as the world does. The weapons we fight with are not the weapons of the world. On the contrary, they have divine power to demolish strongholds. We demolish arguments and every pretension that sets itself up against the knowledge of God, and we take captive every thought to make it obedient to Christ" (2 Corinthians 10:3-5).

This should give us confidence and compassion. It gives confidence because I realize it is not my brilliance nor my students' goodness that convicts and convinces them. It is God's Spirit. It gives compassion because I realize that it is only because of God's grace that my heart is not rebellious and deceived.

## TAKE-AWAY POINT

Teaching God's Word is spiritual warfare for the minds and souls of God's people. It is being a frontline soldier in God's kingdom advancement. It is participation with Him in accomplishing His purposes. Our weapon in this hostile confrontation is prayer. The teacher of God's Word must be an intercessor for the souls of his students. Like Paul, this teacher will pray:

> *I pray also that the eyes of your heart may be enlightened in*
> *order that you may know the hope to which he has called you,*
> *the riches of his glorious inheritance in the saints, and his*
> *incomparably great power for us who believe. That power is*
> *like the working of his mighty strength, which he exerted in*
> *Christ when he raised him from the dead and seated him at his*
> *right hand in the heavenly realms, far above all rule and*
> *authority, power and dominion, and every title that can be*
> *given, not only in the present age but also in the one to come.*
> *And God placed all things under his feet and appointed him*
> *to be head over everything for the church, which is his body,*
> *the fullness of him who fills everything in every way.*
> —*Ephesians 1:18-23*

The creating power that God exerted to raise Christ from the dead is needed to enlighten the eyes of our hearts and the hearts of our students, and that is exactly what God provides through His Spirit. It is no wonder that Paul explodes in praise to the one who sits in the heavenly realms.

Why would we prattle about our needs and significance when we can praise the one who possesses all rule and authority, power and dominion? Why would we piddle with nonessentials when we can participate in His kingdom advancement?

*Question:* Whose responsibility is it to teach covenant children?

*Answer:* It is the responsibility of the home and church.

*Question:* What is the learning process?

*Answer:* We are to prayerfully teach the biblical information, pray for our students to have understanding, and

pray that they will trust and obey. We do this in dependence on the Holy Spirit to give a loyal heart that pumps spiritual life and vitality to every part of our students' being so that every thought is taken captive to make it obedient to Christ.

---

## BECOMING A COVENANT-KEEPER

1. Read Psalm 78 and look for Jesus by asking the questions:
   • What does this teach me about God's character and His promise?
   • What does this teach me about Jesus, the Mediator of the covenant?
   • What covenant privileges and responsibilities does God give me because of who He is and because of what He has done and is doing for me through Jesus?

2. Pray that God will enable you to "demolish arguments and every pretension that sets itself up against the knowledge of God, and . . . take captive every thought to make it obedient to Christ" (2 Corinthians 10:3-5). Pray this every day for a week and record any strongholds God shows you and any victories as He demolishes these arguments.

3. Pray Ephesians 1:18-23 for those you teach, whether in formal teaching situations or in informal relationships.

## CHRISTIAN EDUCATION IDEA

For many parents, deciding how to educate their children is one of the most emotionally charged decisions they make. The intensity of the decision often isolates a family or groups of families within a church. Families cluster with those who have made the same choice, and clustering can threaten unity in a church. In many situations church leadership takes a hands-off approach to this topic because they do not want to appear to take sides. The result is a higher potential for division because people feel isolated and misunderstood.

In 1989 the Harvester Presbyterian Church in Springfield, Virginia, took a bold step. They recognized the importance of integrating the home, church, and school, and they assumed their responsibility to equip parents to fulfill their covenant responsibility in the home. They hired a director and established Harvester Teaching Services (HTS). The director's first assignment was to design a home-school assistance ministry, but God used that as a catalyst to develop a much broader ministry, which is explained in their brochure:

"Some parents home-school, but every parent is a home educator!" This understanding has dynamic implications for the covenant household and the ministry of the local church.

The household is the center of God's plan. In Deuteronomy 6, we learn that God's plan is accomplished over *generations* through *heart*-level *relationships* that are nurtured in *everyday* life.

The breakdown in many Christian families is indicative of the church's failure to equip parents, especially fathers. . . .

A renewed parent-equipping focus ignites a rediscovery of the church as an extended family. Replacing age-segregated programs with household-based ministry restores vibrancy and relevancy to the ministry of the church to all of its members and to our communities.

Eric Wallace, Director of HTS, writes:

As I developed the home-schooling ministry, it became apparent that the needs of home schoolers were not just academic. . . . I discovered that what home schoolers really need is help with basic issues related to everyday life: relationships in the household, discipline, authority, leadership, roles, priorities, serving one another, being able to apply biblical principles, etc.

But even with what we were doing by providing a resource center, classes, and all the activities that we thought would equip them, the reality is that we were still not able to get to the heart of the issue. Then a . . . discovery took place. . . . We saw that the needs of the home-schooling households were not unique to them! . . . Most parents we work with were not raised in Christian homes and have little understanding of how their faith applies to everyday life. The effects of home schooling are so far-reaching in the relationships in the household that parents need more than a book, class, or videotape to practically understand it. The concepts of Christianity are so foreign to them that they need to see it lived out to understand it enough to apply it in the home. Indeed, many parents have little or no ability to evaluate problems and come to biblical conclusions. . . .

All parents home educate, some home school. . . . From a purely covenantal perspective, this statement is also true of everybody in the church whether they are single, single-parent households, couples without children, teens, children. . . . Stating it this way helped to preclude the divisive wall that typically goes up. The often divisive term of *home schooling* was effectively neutralized, and a bridge of unity was built that helps people focus on the similarities found in households, not their differences. . . .

The four-point paradigm for understanding what it means to be a home educator is from Deuteronomy 6: God's plan is accomplished over *generations* through *heart*-level *relationships* that are nurtured in *everyday* life.

For too long parents have only thought of their teaching responsibility as something that they do every day. This understanding is short-sighted because it ignores the other three components. . . . When parents, whether they home school or not, understand the gravity of this vision, they see even more clearly that they need teaching, discipleship, accountability, and the host of other needs that only the church is ordained to give.

The home education vision is more than a plan for parents working with their children; it is the discipleship plan for the entire church. Ministering to generations through heart-level relationships that are nurtured in everyday life is a discipleship plan for singles, orphans, widows, the divorced, teens—everybody. Thus another bridge was built to help pastors see how a home-education ministry can help develop unity among all of the body of Christ and, most importantly, advance household-based ministry.

HTS resources include seminars, curriculum resources, instructional audio and videotapes on a wide range of topics, magazines and newsletters, books and tapes for children, standardized test administration, monthly support group meetings, quarterly Parents of Teens Luncheons, and consulting for other churches. Two treasures that can be used only at the Resource Center are the American Imprints Collection, a massive collection of original writings of America's forefathers from 1639-1800, and the complete writings of George Washington.

HTS now ministers to over 100 families in their area. It has become an effective outreach ministry. For more information write: Eric Wallace, Director, Harvester Teaching Services, 7800 Rolling Road, Springfield, VA 22153.

# 7

~

# *A Strategy for Christian Education*

## LIVING AND TEACHING
## COVENANTALLY

### A TEACHER

I grew up a rich kid. One of my most treasured memories is of the first time I attended Youth Fellowship on Sunday night in our rural church. The older kids loved it, and before I ever went, I knew I would love it too, based on reports from my older brother and sister. Sometime before I started elementary school, Mama decided I could go and not be too great a distraction.

I will never forget the lesson that night. At the front of our small classroom was a table with a large, shiny metal bowl—I suppose it was a punch bowl—filled with water. Our teacher invited us to the table, cautioning us not to bump it. I was so short that someone pulled a chair for me to stand on so I could see over the rim of the bowl. There we stood, half a dozen kids, staring at this bowl of perfectly calm water, wondering what was to come next.

Our teacher took a pebble and put it in the palm of her hand. She held it out so that we could all examine it and see that it was just a common pebble. Then she dropped it in the water, and the surface of the water became rippled as it reflected the concentric circles of influence made by one small not-so-special pebble in a comparatively large vessel of water.

Then she began to teach. She taught us that one not-so-special man, one common woman, one seemingly insignificant child could radiate the love of Christ throughout his/her community even as the small pebble had influenced a volume of water many times its size. The only condition was that just as the pebble was held in the teacher's hand, so we must be willing to be held in the Master's hand to be used as He sees fit.

That simple illustration was a profound lesson. It was forty years ago, and I have never forgotten it. Experiences like that make me a rich kid; and my assets, like that gem of a memory, do not fail to increase in value.

After the lesson we played Bible games. Too soon it was over, and we stood in a circle, held hands, and recited what our teacher called the watch word: "The LORD watch between me and thee, when we are absent one from another" (Genesis 31:49 KJV). Then we were dismissed with words that I came to expect with mathematical certainty, "You boys, don't be running in the church."

This same woman was the first Vacation Bible School teacher I can remember. When I recited the Child's Catechism, she was my proctor. She was an apt administrator, and many a year she organized the Vacation Bible School. She also taught Sunday school—young children, teenagers, and adult women. She was a teacher, and she taught many lessons. But perhaps of greater significance, she taught many life lessons. She taught lessons called perseverance—keeping the faith even when you want to quit. She taught lessons called compassion—assuming the role of guardian for a mentally handicapped brother who could not look after himself, not just for a weekend but for a lifetime. She taught lessons called dedication—saying what you will do and then doing what you said. She taught lessons called trusting God—even when others would justify you if you did not.

Many times she has heard the question, "Do you as a congregation undertake the responsibility of assisting the parents in the Christian nurture of this child?" I do not think that she ever raised her hand mechanically; rather, with great solemnity, she assumed another responsibility. She understood this responsibility and became a pebble in the Master's hand, ready to be placed where He would put her to radiate the character of Christ.

I am now a husband and father, and the Sunday school superintendent in that same church, which is now a growing suburban church. Mrs. Evelyn Wardlaw is now an eighty-four-year-old widow who never had children of her own. I gratefully acknowledge that she impacted my life for Christ in the past, inspires me today, and will influence me for eternity. As one of her spiritual children, I "rise up and call her blessed" (Proverbs 31:28).

*Soli Deo Gloria.*

—Allen Scott,
Marietta, Georgia

# A Strategy for Christian Education

~

Let's recap what we have learned. The content of the covenant is to be taught in the context of covenant relationships. A covenantal approach to Christian education is a careful handling of the Word so that we teach all of Scripture as God's revelation of Himself, and of His covenant with His people through the Mediator of the covenant. It is an intentional cultivation of covenant relationships among the people of God. It culminates in authentic Christianity as God's people live together in His presence and radiate that reality in all of life. It is so comprehensive and compelling that covenant children are not easily dazzled by the attractions of the world because they have seen Jesus on every page of Scripture, and they have seen the radiant faces of those who live in God's presence. It produces deep-rooted Christians who are prepared to be salt and light in the culture for the sake of Christ's Crown and Covenant.

Now how do we actually bring all this into reality in the local church? We will revisit Psalm 78 for some foundational principles.

## INTEGRITY AND SKILL

*He chose David his servant and took him from the sheep pens; from tending the sheep he brought him to be the shepherd of his people Jacob, of Israel his inheritance. And David shepherded them with integrity of heart; with skillful hands he led them.*

—Psalm 78:70-72

We are to shepherd God's sheep with integrity of heart and with skillful hands. Shepherding God's people involves providing them with green pastures where they can feed on His Word. This must be done with skill and integrity. A low-profile maintenance approach to the educational ministry of the church is simply not acceptable. Yet too often this is what churches offer. Dr. Allen Curry, academic dean and professor of Christian education at Reformed Theological Seminary, writes:

> All too many people look at Christian education from the maintenance point of view. They don't expect very much from it; they aren't sure how it got started, but since it's here, they feel they should keep it going. Although this could be described as a shameful attitude, it is still surprising how well Christian education continues to function within churches, even those with this attitude.[1]

The teacher and the educational program of the home and church must be characterized by diligence and excellence. Enormous energy must be spent crafting programs and training teachers so that God's people are shepherded with integrity and skill. Perhaps you are wondering where you will find capable people for this task. Notice that God found David in the sheep pens. David was not an ivory-tower scholar. He was an unlikely choice. He was an unknown shepherd boy. But his hands were dirty, and his muscles ached from doing shepherd work. Skill and integrity are developed as we do the tedious unnoticed tasks in our local churches.

## TEACHING THEM TO OBEY EVERYTHING

Jesus said that we are to teach our students "to obey *everything*" (Matthew 28:20) He has commanded. Paul gave a formidable example when he said, "I have not hesitated to proclaim to you the *whole* will of God" (Acts 20:27). *Everything* and *whole*—these are very inclusive words.

How can we teach our students to obey all things? How can we possibly teach the whole will of God? Does this mean that every time we teach, we are to begin with Genesis and go through Revelation? The answer is obvious. That would be impossible. But it does mean that our educational program must be skillfully crafted so that the whole will of God is proclaimed. In the church this means that a strong Christian education program is developed and careful oversight is given so that the whole will of God is taught at some point along the way.

When we move to a new pastorate, my husband's practice is to spend several months getting to know people, observing what is happening, and assessing the needs. In one church we were thrilled with the quality of the teachers. From the nursery to the adults, the teachers were capable and committed. But soon we discovered that there was no Christian education committee giving oversight, and each teacher made his or her own choice about what to teach and what curriculum materials to use. No one was aware of the fact that in one age-group, the children were studying the same thing in Sunday school and in the Wednesday night program. Even worse, some materials were being used that were not consistent with the theological standards of the church. Because the teachers were experienced, they made the necessary theological adjustments. The inherent danger was that a particular curriculum could become entrenched and a less astute teacher could be enlisted who would not recognize the theological inconsistencies. This was not a skillfully crafted program. When the people realized what was happening, they were eager to appoint a Christian education committee.

Teaching the whole will of God is an expansive mission, but think how much is included in the educational ministry of the church. The nursery, the children's programs, the youth ministry, adult Bible classes, the Sunday school, the men's ministry, and the women's ministry all come under the Christian education umbrella. It has been estimated that as much as 75 to 90 percent of the church's ministry is under the purview of Christian education.

So the caliber of this huge chunk of the church's ministry will undoubtedly be a strong indicator of the health of the church.

Allen Curry writes:

> The ministry of Christian education affords more people the opportunity to learn to exercise their gifts and serve others in the context of biblical ministry. The vast number of tasks that must be done in the areas of teaching and organization in any Christian education program involves many people. These people are engaged in Christian service.
>
> Christian education also provides the most effective means for preserving people's relationships with the church. The Search Institute did a major study on what was the most important variable in churches where people continued in the church from childhood through adulthood. To no one's surprise, the answer was Christian education.[2]

There are many benefits of a strong Christian education committee planning and implementing a well-orchestrated, well-structured educational program. We will consider ten.

BENEFIT #1

A fine-tuned educational program can reinforce the pulpit ministry of the church. Pastors spend an enormous amount of time preparing a sermon that is delivered one time, yet we know that repetition and reinforcement are necessary for retention. A CE committee can work with the pastor to plan small groups to meet to discuss the sermon and its application to life. The pastor and CE committee can work together to develop themes, implement a Scripture memorization program, teach the history of hymns, and plan celebrations of special seasons on the church calendar. Imagine the impact of a pastor preaching on portions of Scripture that families had memorized and a worship service including hymns that children and adults had studied and memorized.

BENEFIT #2

A coordinated program can give greater assurance that a church is proclaiming the whole will of God and is thus "innocent of the blood of all men" (Acts 20:26). The most efficient way to accomplish this is to begin with the Sunday school. It is shameful that the Sunday school hour is often referred to as the most wasted hour of the week. It should be the centerpiece of the educational ministry. It is easier for people to attend Sunday school than any other classes during the week. They simply come to church an hour earlier (or stay an hour later). A CE committee can select a Sunday school curriculum and then build all other programs around it.

For example, the CE committee may decide they want additional emphasis on foreign missions and on equipping children and teens to minister to others. They can design a Sunday night youth program for this purpose. The children's program could be an M & M Club (missions and ministry) where the children write letters to missionaries, hear missionary stories, get involved in local ministry projects such as visiting retirement homes or homebound members of the church. Each program has a well-defined purpose and helps to accomplish the overall objective of proclaiming the whole will of God.

BENEFIT #3

Curriculum materials can be carefully evaluated for theological consistency and pedagogical excellence. Position papers from publishers should be studied to be sure the materials are consistent with the theological standards of the church. Great Commission Publications, a publisher of Sunday school curricula that follows a covenantal approach, gives the following explanation in a position paper. Notice the emphasis on themes we have discussed—a covenantal perspective of Scripture, a covenantal understanding of our relationships with others in the church, the learning process as seen in Psalm 78, the relationship between home and church, and the development of a comprehensive world and life view. As you read this, also consider the importance of finding a good curriculum and using it throughout your Sunday school. Using different materials in each department is problematic because it is easy to have gaps in the overall plan.

> Many Sunday school teachers . . . are perplexed about their role in the ongoing work of the Sunday school. . . . [Our] curriculum has a goal for every department that furthers the overall design of the curriculum. Perhaps knowing what part you play in the entire plan will make you more comfortable and confident in your teaching. Making an analogy between the curriculum and a string of beads may help you.
>
> In order to put together a string of beads, of course, it is necessary to have the beads first. In the first two departments of our curriculum we present the Bible stories which are the basic components of our entire curriculum—the beads. . . .
>
> Students using the Primary course survey stories from the entire Bible. . . . The student should begin to see what the stories teach and gain some familiarity with how they relate to one another. Chronology is considered in this course, but it is periodically ignored; children at this age are not able to handle it intellectually. This makes the lessons more relevant to the lives of students.
>
> In the Preschool and Primary departments, we are concerned that youngsters not only acquire proper beliefs but also do the duty that God requires of them. So, for instance, much emphasis is put on living in families. Each take-home paper has a message to parents to encourage them to participate in their child's learning.
>
> If you are making a string of beads, you must learn what they are and begin to see how they can be used and something of their potential relationship to each other. Then you can put them in order. The same is true of the Bible stories. The children must develop some facility with these basic parts of the entire curriculum. This is done in the Junior department, which deals with Bible history. Students develop an under-

standing of how God makes himself known to us in the different eras of revelation.

Junior students study the development of the people of God from the Genesis account through the story of the church in Acts.... Students see that it is what Jesus does that makes God's kingdom work. All of the lessons of the course—Old Testament and New—emphasize that Jesus Christ is central to God's kingdom. Junior boys and girls are challenged to become dedicated servants of the Lord Jesus and to experience his transforming work in their lives whether at home, school, or play.

The Junior course helps students to put the beads in order. The holes must line up, and the beads must be in the proper relationship to one another. The children discover the development of the relationships in the history of God's people.

In some ways the Junior High course is the capstone of the curriculum. In the bead analogy it is the string that holds everything together. The unifying concept of the Bible is covenant, and in the Junior High course we trace this concept through the entire Bible.

The notion of covenant is particularly relevant to young teens. Many of them are preparing to publicly profess their faith in Christ.... We cherish the doctrine of the covenant.... It is fitting, therefore, for the youth of the church to study this fundamental doctrine as they prepare to join the church.

Covenant is also important to this age group, because it has to do with relationships. Junior Highs are in the process of sorting out their relationships—whether with peers or parents. Our course defines covenant in terms of the relationship between God and us. He is our God, and we are his people. Just as beads will not hold together without a string, neither will our understanding of the Bible without a grasp of the doctrine of the covenant.

But what good is a string of beads if you never wear them? Our Senior High material addresses that point. Once the beads are examined, put in order and strung together, then they should be worn. But how?

A maturing Christian knows how the Bible directs him in all areas of life. So our Senior High course addresses the topic of maturity. In three ways it attempts to show what characterizes a mature Christian. A mature Christian is committed to serving the triune God. He is also committed to serving others. His final commitment is to being the person God created him to be. As a creature of God, he is to use his gifts and skills in whatever God calls him to do.

A string of beads should enhance those who wear them. Likewise the study of God's Word should enable us to serve God better. That is the goal of the ... curriculum. We want students to know what to believe about God and to be equipped to carry out whatever duty God requires of them.[3]

This principle of curriculum continuity should also be applied to the selection of materials for adult classes.

BENEFIT #4

Care can be given to integrating the educational program with the entire ministry-philosophy and ministry-map of the church. The educational program should help achieve the vision and goals of the church. It is the vehicle to teach the vision to the people and to mobilize them to accomplish the goals of the church.

BENEFIT #5

Teachers can be enlisted, trained, and encouraged. Teachers often become discouraged because they feel isolated and inconsequential. The story is told that during the Middle Ages, a dispatcher went out to determine how laborers felt about their work. He went to a building site in France, approached a worker, and asked, "What are you doing?"

The worker snapped, "Are you blind? I'm cutting these impossible boulders with primitive tools and putting them together the way the boss tells me. I'm sweating under this blazing sun; it's backbreaking work, and it's boring."

The dispatcher went to a second worker and asked the same question. This worker replied, "I'm shaping these boulders into usable forms, which are to be assembled according to the architect's plans. It's hard work, and sometimes it gets repetitive, but I earn enough to support the wife and kids. It's a job. Could be worse."

Somewhat encouraged, the dispatcher went to a third worker and again asked, "What are you doing?"

This worker looked at him with sparkling eyes and lifted his arms to the sky as he said, "Why, can't you see? I'm building a cathedral!"[4] When times are planned for teachers to meet together to be challenged with the grand vision of proclaiming the whole will of God, to celebrate what the Lord is doing in their classes, and to pray together, they can stay focused on the cathedrals rather than on the boulders.

### BENEFIT #6

Each teacher can concentrate on his or her particular slice of the educational pie if he or she has a clear picture of the overarching Christian education plan and the particular purpose of the program each is working in. Knowing what students learn in every other program and what they will learn in coming years gives teachers a sense of freedom and focus.

### BENEFIT #7

Community can be cultivated within each class. Leadership teams can be appointed and trained to assimilate new members, plan for fellowship times, minister to needs among class members, follow up with members who are absent, and plan ministry projects. Teams of parents can be appointed for the children's classes. Regular training and meetings can maintain momentum and build in accountability. High visibility for this effort can be achieved as newsletter articles highlight what various classes are doing. Theological integrity can be maintained as sermons and newsletter articles continually teach the biblical basis of community.

BENEFIT #8

Community can be intentionally cultivated between age-groups. Plans can be made and implemented to match classes of children with adults and to assign various ministry projects. An adult and a children's class can be assigned a missionary to pray for and a homebound member to encourage. As the two groups work together, relationships are developed and matured that help the church to maintain a holy fellowship.

BENEFIT #9

People can be trained and mobilized for mercy ministries. Little children, teens, and adults can learn how to enfold the handicapped and how to pray for the oppressed. They can bring food for the poor and write letters to those in prison. They can be given opportunities to learn how "to act justly and to love mercy and to walk humbly with your God" (Micah 6:8).

BENEFIT #10

Unity can be nurtured. The current trend toward highly specialized, age-specific ministries can create division. Every ministry base is covered, often with a staff person over each ministry, but in many cases we would be hard-pressed to call it a team. In fact, often each ministry becomes territorial and actually begins competing with other ministries for space in the church bulletin, dates on the church calendar, and dollars in the budget. When ministries compete, relationships are damaged. Surely this grieves the heart of Jesus who prayed, "May they be brought to complete unity to let the world know that you sent me and have loved them even as you have loved me" (John 17:23).

Since so much of the church's ministry is under the Christian education umbrella, there must be unity among each individual "spoke" of the umbrella, or the work and witness of the church will be defaced. Unity will be characterized by trust and maturity in the relationships because the unity centers around God's glory rather than the needs of any particular group.

Each "spoke," or ministry, should be represented on the CE committee, and they should have regular meetings where vision is developed, goals are set, and overlaps are dealt with in a spirit of love. When there is coordination, cooperation, and accountability to one another, each ministry will be richer, and unity will be deeper. The children's ministry director can enlist the help and prayer support of the women's ministry and the men's ministry to help with children of single parents. The director of women's ministries can work with the youth director to enlist teens to do yard work for widows. The possibilities are endless, and the unity is extraordinary.

## THEOLOGICAL CONSISTENCY AND STRUCTURAL COORDINATION

Theological consistency is essential if we are going to teach the whole will of God with integrity of heart. When there is no theological basis and vision, a ministry will quickly become event and project driven. People are not energized for the long haul by events and projects. Christ's Crown and Covenant give theological integrity and elicit lasting commitment from God's people.

Structural coordination is essential if we are going to teach the whole will of God with skillful hands. Christ's Crown and Covenant are worthy of excellence in all of our planning and in the execution of our plans. Christ's Crown and Covenant inspire us with a sense of awe and wonder because they remind us of the transcendence of God.

I was writing this chapter on an airplane. I was oblivious to the sight below until the young man next to me tapped me on the arm and said, "Isn't it beautiful?" He pointed to the view. I sensed a childlike wonder in his voice, and I asked if it was his first flight. We began to talk about the perspective of God's world when you are soaring high above it. I discovered that he was a college senior preparing to graduate with a degree in special education. I also discovered that he was a Christian. I thanked him for reminding me of the beauty that I almost missed because I was so intent on the task. We must soar high to maintain this sense of wonder and awe.

People of prayer soar . . . they live in God's presence . . . they bask in His splendor . . . and they radiate His presence. Skill and integrity are fashioned in the place of prayer. Jehoshaphat soared. The lessons he learned are the lessons that will undergird a ministry.

## PRAISE, NOT PANIC

In 2 Chronicles 18 Jehoshaphat resorted to eye-level tactics. He rejected the prophet's warning, acted independently, entered into an alliance with Ahab, and barely escaped death. Apparently he learned the lesson we all need to know: "This is the word of the LORD. . . 'Not by might nor by power, but by my Spirit,' says the LORD Almighty" (Zechariah 4:6). In 2 Chronicles 20 Jehoshaphat soars to new heights. He put his trust in God and acted as a part of the covenant community.

When Jehoshaphat was told that a vast army was coming against him, he was alarmed, but this time he did not view the military threat from an eye-level perspective. Neither did he act independently.

> *Jehoshaphat resolved to inquire of the LORD, and he proclaimed a fast for all Judah. The people of Judah came together to seek help from the LORD; indeed, they came from every town in Judah to seek him.*
>
> *—2 Chronicles 20:3-4*

This was a covenantal assembly.

*All the men of Judah, with their wives and children and little*
*ones, stood there before the LORD.*
                                              —*2 Chronicles 20:13*

Jehoshaphat prayed to the God of covenant faithfulness. This
is one of the great prayers of Scripture.

*Then Jehoshaphat stood up in the assembly of Judah and*
*Jerusalem at the temple of the LORD in the front of the new*
*courtyard and said:*
    *"O LORD, God of our fathers, are you not the God who*
*is in heaven? You rule over all the kingdoms of the nations.*
*Power and might are in your hand, and no one can with-*
*stand you. O our God, did you not drive out the inhabi-*
*tants of this land before your people Israel and give it*
*forever to the descendants of Abraham your friend? They*
*have lived in it and have built in it a sanctuary for your*
*Name, saying, 'If calamity comes upon us, whether the*
*sword of judgment, or plague or famine, we will stand in*
*your presence before this temple that bears your Name and*
*will cry out to you in our distress, and you will hear us and*
*save us.'*
    *"But now here are men from Ammon, Moab and Mount*
*Seir, whose territory you would not allow Israel to invade*
*when they came from Egypt; so they turned away from them*
*and did not destroy them. See how they are repaying us by*
*coming to drive us out of the possession you gave us as an*
*inheritance. O our God, will you not judge them? For we have*
*no power to face this vast army that is attacking us. We do not*
*know what to do, but our eyes are upon you."*
                                            —*2 Chronicles 20:5-12*

Following Jehoshaphat's prayer, the Spirit of the LORD came
upon Jahaziel, and he stood before the assembly and said:

*"Listen, King Jehoshaphat and all who live in Judah and Jerusalem! This is what the LORD says to you: 'Do not be afraid or discouraged because of this vast army. For the battle is not yours, but God's. Tomorrow march down against them. They will be climbing up by the Pass of Ziz, and you will find them at the end of the gorge in the Desert of Jeruel. You will not have to fight this battle. Take up your positions; stand firm and see the deliverance the LORD will give you, O Judah and Jerusalem. Do not be afraid; do not be discouraged. Go out to face them tomorrow, and the LORD will be with you.'"*
—2 Chronicles 20:15-17

Notice the seeming incongruity of Jahaziel's words. He tells them the battle is not theirs, but in the very next breath tells them to march, to take up their positions, and to stand firm. What is the proper position when a vast army is coming against us? We can look to Jehoshaphat's moment in history and learn from him.

*Jehoshaphat bowed with his face to the ground, and all the people of Judah and Jerusalem fell down in worship before the LORD.*
—2 Chronicles 20:18

The relevancy of this lesson from antiquity cannot be over-stated. When a vast army is coming against us, here is the strategy. Gather other believers and pray Jehoshaphat's prayer. Then bow before our Sovereign in worship.

The story gets better! As the vast army advances toward them . . .

*. . . some Levites from the Kohathites and Korahites stood up and praised the LORD, the God of Israel, with very loud voice. Early in the morning they left for the Desert of Tekoa. As they set out, Jehoshaphat stood and said, "Listen to me, Judah and people of Jerusalem! Have faith in the LORD your God and you will be upheld; have faith in his prophets and you will be successful."*
—2 Chronicles 20:19-20

Jehoshaphat consults the people and then executes the most bizarre military tactic I have ever heard of. Rather than putting his strongest tanks in the front . . .

> *Jehoshaphat appointed men to sing to the LORD and to praise him for the splendor of his holiness as they went out at the head of the army, saying: "Give thanks to the LORD, for his love endures forever."*
>
> —*2 Chronicles 20:21*

Can you imagine such a spectacle? If there were enemy scouts watching them, think about their reconnaissance report. But for one who is thinking covenantally, this is not at all peculiar. These covenant people simply stood on the shoulders of those who had gone before them, and they saw the situation from a covenantal perspective. In this particular instance, they stood on Solomon's shoulders. They sang the very words that had been sung at the completion of the temple. And surely they anticipated the same result. Rewind the historical clock about a hundred years to get the mental picture of what Jehoshaphat must have had in his mind. In 2 Chronicles 5:13-14 we read:

> *The trumpeters and singers joined in unison, as with one voice, to give praise and thanks to the LORD. Accompanied by trumpets, cymbals and other instruments, they raised their voices in praise to the LORD and sang:*
> *"He is good; his love endures forever."*
> *Then the temple of the LORD was filled with a cloud, and the priests could not perform their service because of the cloud, for the glory of the LORD filled the temple of God.*

Jehoshaphat's strategy is not really bizarre. He does not panic. . . . He leads the people in praise to the King of kings because he knows from history that praise is the proper approach to God's presence. The psalmist says it beautifully:

*Enter his gates with thanksgiving and his courts with praise; give thanks to him and praise his name. For the LORD is good and his love endures forever; his faithfulness continues through all generations.*

—*Psalm 100:4-5*

I love this story. It keeps getting better. Jehoshaphat and his army are on the move. They cannot see the enemy yet, but . . .

*As they began to sing and praise, the LORD set ambushes against the men of Ammon and Moab and Mount Seir who were invading Judah, and they were defeated. The men of Ammon and Moab rose up against the men from Mount Seir to destroy and annihilate them. After they finished slaughtering the men from Seir, they helped to destroy one another.*

—*2 Chronicles 20:22-23*

Then God's covenant people come to the top of the hill that looks out over the desert, expecting to see the vast army, but "they saw only dead bodies lying on the ground; no one had escaped" (verse 24).

It still gets better . . .

*So Jehoshaphat and his men went to carry off their plunder, and they found among them a great amount of equipment and clothing and also articles of value—more than they could take away. There was so much plunder that it took three days to collect it.*

—*2 Chronicles 20:25*

Despite the odds from an eye-level perspective, they thought, prayed, and acted covenantally. They advanced not in their own strength, but in total dependence on the Lord. And it took three days to gather the loot. It is no wonder that they called the place the Valley of Beracah, which means blessing.

The conclusion:

*Then, led by Jehoshaphat, all the men of Judah and Jerusalem returned joyfully to Jerusalem, for the LORD had given them cause to rejoice over their enemies. They entered Jerusalem and went to the temple of the LORD with harps and lutes and trumpets. The fear of God came upon all the kingdoms of the countries when they heard how the LORD had fought against the enemies of Israel. And the kingdom of Jehoshaphat was at peace, for his God had given him rest on every side.*
—2 Chronicles 20:27-30

We often face a vast army. Sometimes it is discouragement. Sometimes it is fear because we feel overwhelmed with the responsibility of kingdom work. Sometimes it is doubt—should I really encourage this young person to obey God's Word regardless of the consequences? Sometimes it is a heavy burden for an unsaved person in our class or a wayward covenant child. Sometimes it is a conflict that threatens to disrupt the unity of the covenant community. Sometimes it is fatigue. Sometimes it is the dark oppression of spiritual warfare. Many times Jehoshaphat's prayer is my prayer: "I have no power. . . . I do not know what to do . . . but my eyes are upon You." Then I find that I enter His presence as I stand upon the shoulders of Solomon and Jehoshaphat and say repeatedly: "He is good; his love endures forever."

I have learned that I stand more firmly if I ask others to stand with me—that is the covenant way. The blessings to be collected are far more valuable and more lasting than gold and silver.

TAKE-AWAY POINT

Where will we find people with vision and passion to shepherd people with skillful hands and integrity of heart? Look in the sheep pens. Look for those who are doing it. Call them out, equip them, encourage them, celebrate them.

Don't settle for mediocrity. Soar high in the place of prayer, and then go forth in a spirit of praise to the Valley of Beracah and gather the blessing of God anointing your efforts with His grace. In commenting on the power of praise, a Scottish divine said:

> At the dedication of the temple, many prayers were made, and many sacrifices offered, without any tokens of divine acceptance. But when singers and players on instruments began, as one, to make one sound to be heard in praising and thanking the Lord, saying, "For He is good, for His mercy endureth forever," then the glory of the Lord descended and filled the temple.[5]

---
∾
---

*Question:* How do we plan for and implement a Christian education ministry in the church?

*Answer:* A Christian education committee should skillfully develop a comprehensive plan so that the whole counsel of God is taught with theological and relational integrity. The plan, the programs, and the people must be saturated with prayer.

---

BECOMING A COVENANT-KEEPER

1. Read and meditate on Psalm 100.

2. Read and meditate on 2 Chronicles 20. Think about the vast armies you face and pray Jehoshaphat's prayer.

3. Reread the quote from the Scottish divine at the end of the chapter and pray that you will view all of life from a praise perspective.

4. Look back at the benefits of a well-planned Christian education program. Thank God for those who are working in this area of ministry in your church. Consider how you can encourage them. Pray about whether God would have you join them.

## CHRISTIAN EDUCATION IDEA

Below are some practical ideas to help a Christian education committee develop a strong program with integrity and skill.

1.  All segments of the CE program should be represented on the committee so that those who are doing the work have input into the decisions. It may also be helpful to have people with educational training on the committee.

2.  The committee should know the vision and goals of the elders (or governing body) of the church. There should also be a specific vision/purpose statement for the CE committee.

3.  The chairman of the committee should put energy into developing a spirit of unity and support among the committee members. An atmosphere should be cultivated where everyone can speak openly and honestly without fearing attack from other committee members. There should be a commitment from every member of the committee to pray for one another, to prayerfully seek what is best for the whole program and not just one part of the program, to be respectful to each other, to maintain confidentiality, and once decisions are made, to leave the meeting with "one voice." The chairman should not allow one or two to dominate discussions. Sometimes simply going around and asking everyone for a thirty-second summary of their thoughts changes the course of a discussion. *The Peacemaker* by Ken Sande is an excellent resource to learn biblical procedures for dealing with conflict.

4.  Assess the needs and opportunities by evaluating what programs are in place, what curriculum is being used in each program, and determining any gaps. Then design programs with a clearly defined purpose and find materials that will help achieve that purpose.

5.  Consider having a CE theme that will give focus to the programs. (See Christian Education Idea at the end of chapter 2.)

6.  Reread the Christian Education Idea sections after each chapter and see if any would strengthen your program.

7.  Reread the benefits listed in this chapter and discuss their applicability to your program.

8.  When teachers are recruited, give a clear written description of the purpose of the program, the curriculum to be used, the expectations of the teacher, and the commitment from the committee of their prayer support.

9.  Provide a time of teacher training when the covenantal approach is presented. Help the committee members and the teachers keep a covenantal perspective by preparing a handout with the following:
    Questions teachers should ask about every lesson to help teach the content of the covenant:
    • What does this teach about the character of God?
    • What does this teach about Jesus, the Mediator of the covenant?
    • What are the covenant privileges and responsibilities that would apply to my students?
    Questions teachers should ask about every lesson, activity, project, and event to be sure it is building community in at least one area:
    • How does this build community in our class?
    • How does it build community with other members of our church?
    • How does it advance God's kingdom in the world?
    *(The Leader's Guide for this book is written to help teachers integrate these two sets of questions into the lessons. The ideas and format in this Guide can be used in teaching other studies.)*

10. Frequently communicate with teachers through teacher gatherings and written memos, reminding them of the above questions and of the CE theme. At gatherings have teachers give testimonies of how they are doing this and the effect among their students.

11. Have yearly evaluations of each program to be sure it is accomplishing its purpose and that the stated purpose is still applicable.

# 8

*The Villagers
and the Village Life*

$$\approx$$

## LIVING AND TEACHING
## COVENANTALLY

### GRANNY

Ten years ago there was a youth group made up of covenant kids who knew most of the answers! Into this smart, creative, verbal, cocky, know-it-all group of senior highs came Granny (aka Penny Pappas). Her first Sunday among us found us slouching on an old couch. Granny asked that we join her around the table. One of our sharp young men threw down a challenge. "Why?" he asked. Perhaps this would be a good time to tell you that Granny and John Pappas raised four children; she also had been a teacher and principal of our Christian school. Needless to say, she was not thrown by our reluctant spirits or our questioning, smarty attitudes.

Granny taught us many things. First of all, she was genuinely concerned with each one of us—she cared about what we said and what we thought. We quickly learned she was here because the elders of our church had asked her and, more importantly, because the Lord had given her a love for this unlovely group. She set parameters, and we learned proper etiquette, respect for authority, and patience with one another, as well as clear teaching from the Word of God.

To foster servants' hearts in us, Granny regularly volunteered us for duty in the church—such as serving at family night dinners, visiting and doing chores for the elderly, and helping in the nursery. This group of teenagers became very adept at assisting Granny as she catered weddings in our church. There was no job we couldn't tackle—decorating tables, flower arrangements, parking cars, and even chopping and cooking in the kitchen.

Our times together included many fun things. Granny and her

husband had a wonderful country home filled with antiques, a full cooking fireplace in the kitchen, and a warm atmosphere that made all who entered feel loved and appreciated. In this home Granny entertained us on New Year's Eve. There were ground rules: The girls had to dress in their prom dresses and the boys in suits or tuxedos. We ate from her fine china, she and her husband prepared the dinner and served us, and we enjoyed feeling quite grown-up and special! Other times she and John invited our parents to dinner to discuss the things we were being taught in Sunday school. Granny worked very hard to keep the lines of communication open between all of us.

Occasionally Granny digressed from our regular Sunday school curriculum to discuss special topics. One such diversion was a series on dating, marriage, and sexual ethics. We looked at biblical principles, invited older members of the church body to serve on a panel, and we were able to ask them hard questions about the temptations they faced when they were our ages. This had several beneficial results. First, it was helpful to learn from the experiences of our elders, who were quite candid with us. Second, it helped us bridge the generation gap, share with one another, and see each other in a different light.

We began to change. Her persistent teaching and modeling paid off. A deep love, respect, and appreciation for Granny developed, which continues to this very day. There now are eight twenty-three- to twenty-six-year-olds who are more biblically equipped adults with a more comprehensive worldview because of this remarkable woman.

My testimony is a tribute to God's faithfulness *and* to His use of Penny Pappas, who was willing to come out of retirement for another round of kingdom service.

—Rob Patete,
Miami, Florida

# The Villagers
# and the Village Life

~

God's covenant relationship with us is to be mirrored in our relationships with one another. God tells us this in His Word, and He showed us what it looks like in the person of Jesus. Show and tell is a powerful method of teaching.

We all show and tell what we believe all the time.

Sometimes we show and tell biblical truth. Sometimes we tell biblical truth and show untruth. If we think we are saying and showing nothing, that silence and passivity is its own message.

In the covenant village, there is a sense in which all of the villagers are teachers and all are students all the time. Of course the teacher/student relationship is closer and more intentional in formal teaching situations, but the principles in the following discussion apply to all. They apply in the home and in the church as we show and tell what we believe.

## THE TEACHER

Jesus said, "A student is not above his teacher, but everyone who is fully trained will be like his teacher" (Luke 6:40). One interesting thing about this statement is that Jesus did not say whether this is a good thing or a bad thing. It just happens. To some degree, students will become like their teachers.

No wonder James wrote, "Not many of you should presume to be teachers, my brothers, because you know that we who teach will be judged more strictly" (James 3:1).

Paul encourages us not to back away from this calling when he boldly says, "Follow my example, as I follow the example of Christ" (1 Corinthians 11:1).

Jesus cautioned and challenged us when He said, "Anyone who breaks one of the least of these commandments and teaches others to do the same will be called least in the kingdom of heaven, but whoever practices and teaches these commands will be called great in the kingdom of heaven" (Matthew 5:19).

Those who are committed to Christ's Crown and Covenant are compelled to share that passion with others by practicing and teaching His commands. Some do this through nurturing relationships in informal situations. Some do it in formal situations. They can't help themselves. Their hearts burn to tell others that Jesus is alive and to show it in the way they live.

As we explore some ways that we can become more effective teachers, be aware that this discussion has more to do with principles than with methods. Thus it is applicable to all ages and all relationships. It applies to my relationship with our adult children, our grandchildren, the students in my Sunday school class, and the children and adults I interact with at church. So how do we do it?

First, we must ask the question: What is my goal for my students? Paul provides the answer: "We proclaim him, admonishing and teaching everyone with all wisdom, so that we may present everyone perfect in Christ. To this end I labor, struggling with all his energy, which so powerfully works in me" (Colossians 1:28-29).

Immediately we are confronted with the reality that this is a huge investment of time and emotional energy. The word translated "labor" is the Greek word *kopiano*, which means to toil, to grow weary. The word translated "perfect" is the Greek word *teleios*, which means having reached its end, complete, mature. We must never settle for anything less than maturity in Christ, which means that we will never be through teaching because our students will not reach final perfection until they are glorified in heaven. That is the ultimate goal—to present a student to our Father to whom He can say, "Well done, good and faithful servant! . . . Come and share your master's happiness!" (Matthew 25:23).

Second, we must continually remind ourselves of the content/context principle. Biblical truth is to be taught in the context of a loving relationship. Paul emphasized this to young Timothy. Just before his charge to "preach the Word" (2 Timothy 4:2), Paul reminded Timothy about *what* he had been taught and *who* had taught him. Dr. Allen Curry has said that Paul reminded him of his text and his teachers.

> *But as for you, continue in what you have learned and have become convinced of, because you know those from whom you learned it, and how from infancy you have known the holy Scriptures, which are able to make you wise for salvation through faith in Christ Jesus. All Scripture is God-breathed and is useful for teaching, rebuking, correcting and training in righteousness, so that the man of God may be thoroughly equipped for every good work.*
>
> *—2 Timothy 3:14-17*

Timothy was a covenant child. His teachers were his grandmother Lois, his mother Eunice, and Paul himself. These three had invested themselves in Timothy. Timothy had been taught the language of faith from infancy. He had moved all the way through the learning process to trust and obedience. He became personally convinced of what he had been taught. As he now embarks on his own ministry of teaching, Paul reminds him of the content/context synthesis. He reminds him of the authority of Scripture and the trustworthiness of those who taught him. Paul is teaching Timothy, and us, that we are responsible to obey God's Word because it is the very Word of the living God. Regardless of the obedience or disobedience of the teachers, we must obey the Word because it is our authority. It is our rule for faith and practice. But Timothy had the huge advantage of being able to remember that those who taught it to him lived it before him. Paul then challenged Timothy to do no less for his students.

> *In the presence of God and of Christ Jesus, who will judge the living and the dead, and in view of his appearing and his kingdom, I give you this charge: Preach the Word; be prepared in season and out of season; correct, rebuke and encourage— with great patience and careful instruction.*
>
> *—2 Timothy 4:1-2*

A teacher can dislike math and dislike his students and still teach them math. But I can never teach God's Word "in the presence of God and of Christ Jesus, who will judge the living and the dead, and in view of his appearing and his kingdom" in an impersonal, indifferent manner. Teaching the Bible involves sharing what God's Spirit is teaching us and enabling us to apply in our own lives. It is intensely personal.

Third, sprinkled throughout his letters to Timothy, Paul gives some traits of a faithful teacher. We must prayerfully ask God to increasingly build these traits into our lives.

Teacher Trait #1: A living faith. "I have been reminded of your sincere faith, which first lived in your grandmother Lois and in your mother Eunice and, I am persuaded, now lives in you also" (2 Timothy 1:5).

Teacher Trait #2: Diligent student of the Word. "Do your best to present yourself to God as one approved, a workman who does not need to be ashamed and who correctly handles the word of truth" (2 Timothy 2:15).

Teacher Trait #3: Example of godliness. "Set an example for the believers in speech, in life, in love, in faith and in purity. . . . Devote yourself to the public reading of Scripture, to preaching and to teaching. . . . Be diligent in these matters; give yourself wholly to them, so that everyone may see your progress. Watch your life and doctrine closely. Persevere in them, because if you do, you will save both yourself and your hearers" (1 Timothy 4:12-16).

Teacher Trait #4: A grateful servant spirit. "I thank Christ Jesus our Lord, who has given me strength, that he considered me faithful, appointing me to his service" (1 Timothy 1:12).

Teacher Trait #5: A constant awareness of our own sinfulness and God's mercy. "Even though I was once a blasphemer and a persecutor and a violent man, I was shown mercy because I acted in ignorance and unbelief. The grace of our Lord was poured out on me abundantly, along with the faith and love that are in Christ Jesus. Here is a trustworthy saying that deserves full acceptance: Christ Jesus came into the world to save sinners—of whom I am the worst" (1 Timothy 1:13-15).

Teacher Trait #6: A disciple maker. "And the things you have heard me say in the presence of many witnesses entrust to reliable men who will also be qualified to teach others" (2 Timothy 2:2).

Teacher Trait #7: A unity builder. "Flee the evil desires of youth, and pursue righteousness, faith, love and peace, along with those who call on the Lord out of a pure heart. Don't have anything to do with foolish and stupid arguments, because you know they produce quarrels. And the Lord's servant must not quarrel; instead, he must be kind to everyone, able to teach, not resentful. Those who oppose him he must gently instruct, in the hope that God will grant them repentance leading them to a knowledge of the truth, and that they will come to their senses and escape from the trap of the devil, who has taken them captive to do his will" (2 Timothy 2:22-26).

Teacher Trait #8: A heart for evangelism. "But you, keep your head in all situations, endure hardship, do the work of an evangelist. . . ." (2 Timothy 4:5).

Paul and Timothy provide a positive example that "everyone who is fully trained will be like his teacher" (Luke 6:40). Timothy is so like Paul. The teacher/student relationship is scary. Our influence over others is awesome. It is also wonderful. "Those who are wise will shine like the brightness of the heavens, and those who lead many to righteousness, like the stars for ever and ever" (Daniel 12:3).

Paul's testimony of his strong commitment to his students should surely spur us on to follow his example because he followed the example of Jesus. ". . . But we were gentle among you, like a mother caring for her little children. We loved you so much that we were delighted to share with you not only the gospel of God but our lives as well, because you had become so dear to us" (1 Thessalonians 2:7-8).

I can almost hear your groans because I hear the protests of my own heart: *I cannot possibly do this.* Our Savior knows that, and He made provision for it. Apparently Paul knew that Timothy would have the same uncertainty because, as he challenged him, he reminded him of the provision: "Guard the good deposit that was entrusted to you—guard it with the help of the Holy Spirit who lives in us" (2 Timothy 1:14).

It is the Holy Spirit who will be our Counselor and Teacher (John 14:15-26). He will produce in us what we cannot produce in ourselves: ". . . The fruit of the Spirit is love, joy, peace, patience, kindness, goodness, faithfulness, gentleness and self-control" (Galatians 5:22-23). The Spirit of Truth who enables our students to believe truth also enables us to believe, live, and speak truth.

## THE STUDENT

Following the episode of Mary and Joseph leaving the boy Jesus in Jerusalem and frantically searching for Him until they find Him in the temple teaching the teachers, we read: "Then he went down to Nazareth with them and was obedient to them. But his mother treasured all these things in her heart. And Jesus grew in wisdom and stature, and in favor with God and men" (Luke 2:51-52).

Our children need to grow in the same four areas that Jesus grew. But notice the context in which this growth took place—parents who loved and a child who obeyed. We must maintain loving authority in our homes/classrooms; nurture covenant relationships with our students; and provide instruction, application, and opportunities for them to develop in wisdom, stature, favor with God and favor with man. The four growth areas have application to all ages.

The Hebrew word for "wise," *hakam*, means more than knowledge or intelligence. It means the right use of knowledge. It involves a way of thinking about and reacting to life experiences. The wisdom of the Old Testament is a worldview that differs from other ancient worldviews, because it reflects the teaching of a personal God who is holy, righteous, and just and who expects those living in covenant relationship with Him to reflect His character in the practical affairs of life. We might define wisdom as knowing what God wants me to know, thinking the way God wants me to think, and doing what God wants me to do. The psalmist said, "The fear of the Lord is the beginning of wisdom; all who follow his precepts have good understanding" (Psalm 111:10).

To grow in stature certainly has to do with physical growth, but the Hebrew word *helikia* also means "maturity."

The word translated "favor" is the Greek word *charis*, which means "grace." To grow in God's favor is to grow in His grace. John said it succinctly: "He must become greater; I must become less" (John 3:30). There must be less of me so that there can be more of Christ. He made provision for this. "He himself bore our sins in his body on the tree, so that we might die to sins and live for righteousness; by his wounds you have been healed" (1 Peter 2:24). The more we are filled with His grace, the more we can touch one another with that grace and thus grow in favor with God and man.

Growth in wisdom, stature, favor with God and favor with man all combine to achieve the goal Paul envisioned for his students— to present them perfect or mature in Christ (Colossians 1:28).

In *A Quest for Godliness: The Puritan Vision of the Christian Life*, J. I. Packer profiles Puritan maturity. This description provides a benchmark for us as we labor with all our energy to instill God's truth in our students.

> Maturity is a compound of wisdom, goodwill, resilience, and creativity. The Puritans exemplified maturity. . . . They were great souls serving a great God. In them clear-headed passion and warm-hearted compassion combined. Visionary and practical, idealistic and realistic too, goal-oriented and

methodical, they were great believers, great hopers, great doers, and great sufferers. But their sufferings . . . seasoned and ripened them till they gained a stature that was nothing short of heroic. Ease and luxury, such as our affluence brings us today, do not make for maturity; hardship and struggle however do, and the Puritans' battles against the spiritual and climatic wildernesses in which God set them produced a virility of character, undaunted and unsinkable, rising above discouragement and fears. . . .[1]

Packer then suggests some lessons we can learn from the Puritans' maturity. These are marks of maturity that we can teach our students.

First, there are lessons for us in *the integration of their daily lives*. As their Christianity was all-embracing, so their living was all of a piece. . . . All creation, so far as they were concerned, was sacred, and all activities, of whatever kind, must be sanctified, that is, done to the glory of God. . . .

Second, there are lessons for us in *the quality of their spiritual experience*. In the Puritans' communion with God, as Jesus Christ was central, so Holy Scripture was supreme. . . . Puritan meditation on Scripture was modelled on the Puritan sermon; in meditation the Puritan would seek to search and challenge his heart, stir his affections to hate sin and love righteousness, and encourage himself with God's promises. . . .

Third, there are lessons for us in *their passion for effective action*. . . . They were men of action in the pure Reformed mold—crusading activists without a jot of self-reliance; workers for God who depended utterly on God to work in and through them, and who always gave God the praise for anything they did that in retrospect seemed to them to have been right; gifted men who prayed earnestly that God would enable them to use their powers, not for self-display, but for his praise.

Fourth, there are lessons for us in *their program for family stability*. . . . The Puritan ethic of marriage was to look not for a partner whom you *do* love passionately at this moment, but rather for one whom you *can* love steadily as your best friend for life, and then to proceed with God's help to do just that. The Puritan ethic of nurture was to train up children in the way they should go, to care for their bodies and souls together, and to educate them for sober, godly, socially useful adult living. . . .

Fifth, there are lessons to be learned from their *sense of human worth*. Through believing in a great God . . . they gained a vivid awareness of the greatness of moral issues, of eternity, and of the human soul. . . .

Sixth, there are lessons to be learned from the Puritans' *ideal of church renewal*. . . . "renewal" was not a word that they used; they spoke only of "reformation" and "reform.". . . The essence of this kind of "reformation" was enrichment of understanding of God's truth, arousal of affections God-ward, increase of ardour in one's devotions, and more love, joy, and firmness of Christian purpose in one's calling and personal life. . . . the ideal for the church was that . . . all the members of each congregation should be "reformed"— brought, that is, by God's grace without disorder into a state of what we would call revival, so as to be truly and thoroughly converted, theologically orthodox and sound, spiritually alert and expectant, in character terms wise and steady, ethically enterprising and obedient, and humbly but joyously sure of their salvation. . . .[2]

Granted the culture we live in makes it difficult to entice our students to pursue this kind of maturity. But the real obstacle is not the culture; it is the bent of the heart toward selfism. However, this gives great hope. As long as we are in this world, the culture will be against us, but the heart can be radically and instantaneously changed by the power of the Holy Spirit. Our part is to be aware of the pull of sin and not accommodate it, but strive against it. Whether our students are five or fifty, we must understand that both "they" and "we" are sinners.

S. G. DeGraaf wrote:

> The typical sin of the child is putting himself first. The child
> has room in his life for God—as long as God comes second.
> Are we acting responsibly when we accommodate ourselves
> to this sinful inclination on the part of children? Or should we
> oppose it? Admittedly, grasping the Bible story from the
> proper point of view is very difficult for the child, not because
> his understanding is limited but because his heart says no.
> Little children have no more room for God in their lives than
> adults. If we make those children see God's centrality in
> human life, we will have reached our main goal. . . .[3]

Much of the emphasis today is on meeting our students' needs.
The four growth areas we see in Luke 2:51-52 (wisdom, maturity,
favor with God, favor with man) are not inward focused. If we are
going to challenge our students to aspire to biblical maturity, we
must continually confront them with the holiness of God and the
reality of their own sin.

Dr. Edward Welch, a member of the staff of the Christian
Counseling and Educational Foundation in Philadelphia, in his
book entitled *When People Are Big and God Is Small*, guides us to a
God-centered approach regarding issues such as self-esteem and a
needs-approach to ministry. He writes:

> When needs, rather than sin, are seen as our primary problem,
> not only is our self-understanding affected, but the gospel
> itself is changed.
>     . . . The essence of imaging God is to rejoice in God's pres-
> ence, to love him above all else, and to live for his glory, not our
> own. The most basic question of human existence becomes
> "How can I bring glory to God?"—not "How will God meet
> my psychological longings?" These differences create very dif-
> ferent tugs on our hearts: one constantly pulls us outward
> toward God, the other first pulls inward toward ourselves. . . .

... to look to Christ to meet our psychological needs is to Christianize our lusts. . . .

Self-serving needs are not meant to be satisfied; they are meant to be put to death.[4]

Dr. Welch explains that a biblical perspective on who we are focuses on the image of God in us. "To be created in the image of God means that we are like God in every way a creature can be like him, to the praise of his glorious grace (Eph. 1:6, 12, 14). This indicates that God has given us gifts to serve rather than needs to be served. Any other perspective is less than biblical and will ultimately lead us toward misery rather than joy."[5]

Any other perspective will also lead our students toward misery rather than joy. A covenantal approach points our students to their Savior rather than to their significance. The more we see Jesus, the more we see our sinfulness. The recognition of sin leads to repentance. The joy of repentance is that it is immediately followed by forgiveness.

In explaining the importance of teaching from a covenantal perspective, S. G. DeGraaf wrote:

The stories will be hard for the children to understand, not because their minds cannot grasp them but because their hearts do not accept them. Because sin has driven us apart, every child is a born individualist. We stand in the world as separate beings and form our opinions on our own.

If you play up to that individualism in telling the stories, the children will readily accept what you say. But can we allow ourselves to be governed by a situation imposed on us by sin and sell the gospel the way an advertiser sells beauty soap? Or should our storytelling try to shatter that individualism?[6]

We must show our students Jesus; we must show them that they are part of the village of faith because they belong to Him; we must show them that they have village duties.

## VILLAGE LIFE

We will use an Old Testament example to consider village life. In Judges 4 and 5 we see the familiar cycle of covenant-breaking by the people, judgment by God, a cry for deliverance, and God's mercy to His children. Judges 4 gives the facts, and Judges 5 provides the doxology. We must take them together to get the full story. There are numerous plots and applications, one of which is a description of the breakdown and restoration of village life. Deborah describes it this way:

> . . . *The roads were abandoned; travelers took to winding paths. Village life in Israel ceased, ceased until I, Deborah, arose, arose a mother in Israel. When they chose new gods, war came to the city gates, and not a shield or spear was seen among forty thousand in Israel.*
>
> —*Judges 5:6-8*

The highways were unsafe for the Israelites because of foreign oppressors and robbers. There was isolation and fear. There was no community identity or solidarity. There was no leadership. The people chose new gods, and the result was no safety and no covenant sanity. Village life ceased, and God's people were demoralized, paralyzed, and vulnerable.

Village life ceased *until*—until God raised up a mother in Israel who had a covenantal perspective of the situation and a covenantal relationship with Yahweh. The story unfolds:

> *After Ehud died, the Israelites once again did evil in the eyes of the LORD. So the LORD sold them into the hands of Jabin, a king of Canaan, who reigned in Hazor. The commander of his army was Sisera. . . . Because he had nine hundred iron chariots and had cruelly oppressed the Israelites for twenty years, they cried to the LORD for help.*
>
> *Deborah, a prophetess, the wife of Lappidoth, was leading Israel at that time. . . . She sent for Barak . . . and said to him,*

*"The LORD, the God of Israel, commands you: 'Go, take with you ten thousand men of Naphtali and Zebulun and lead the way to Mount Tabor. I will lure Sisera, the commander of Jabin's army, with his chariots and his troops to the Kishon River and give him into your hands.'"*

*—Judges 4:1-4, 6-7*

Deborah knew that her word and her strategy would never equip and empower the people to defeat their enemy and to restore village life. When she called to Barak, she made sure he understood that it was the Lord who was the commander and the tactician of this battle. And God did exactly what He promised. As Barak and the troops advanced, a violent thunderstorm threw Sisera's troops into a panic and his nine hundred chariots into the mud. "All the troops of Sisera fell by the sword; not a man was left" (v. 16).

Then Deborah sang a song of praise, and from beginning to end the strong theme is God's covenant faithfulness despite His children's covenant-breaking: "When the princes in Israel take the lead, when the people willingly offer themselves—praise the LORD! Hear this, you kings! Listen, you rulers! I will sing to the LORD, I will sing; I will make music to the LORD, the God of Israel" (Judges 5:2-3).

Deborah begins by reminding her hearers that the victory belongs to the Lord. She knew that it was not her wisdom or Barak's might that had won the battle. It was God's Word and power that gave this resounding victory. If the princes in Israel take the lead and the people follow, it is because of God's grace in them. So it is God who should be praised.

Deborah teaches from a covenantal perspective. She quickly reminds the people of the historic foundation of their covenant relationship with Yahweh: "O LORD, when you went out from Seir, when you marched from the land of Edom, the earth shook, the heavens poured, the clouds poured down water. The mountains quaked before the LORD, the One of Sinai, before the LORD, the God of Israel" (vv. 4-5).

She refers back to Sinai as she praises God for their present deliverance. This would bring to their remembrance the redemptive flow of history, the covenant promise to their forefathers, and their covenant responsibilities as God's chosen people.

Then Deborah gives a vivid description of village life after the defeat of Jabin.

> *My heart is with Israel's princes, with the willing volunteers among the people. Praise the LORD! You who ride on white donkeys, sitting on your saddle blankets, and you who walk along the road, consider the voice of the singers at the watering places. They recite the righteous acts of the LORD, the righteous acts of his warriors in Israel. Then the people of the LORD went down to the city gates.*
>
> *—Judges 5:9-11*

Note the contrast. In verses 6-8 there is no village life. Now there are community leaders. There are willing volunteers. And Deborah quickly reminds them that God is to be praised because He is the one who made their hearts willing. The white donkeys symbolize a return of civil order. The people are no longer in isolation. They freely gather at the watering places and praise God as they recite His righteous acts. This is village life as it should be.

Deborah brings her song to a rousing conclusion by rejoicing in the fact that this kind of village life is the catalyst for the villagers to reflect the one who said, "I am the light of the world" (John 8:12). "'So may all your enemies perish, O LORD! But may they who love you be like the sun when it rises in its strength.' Then the land had peace forty years" (Judges 5:31).

Those who live in God's presence will be like the sun when it is at full strength. They and their village will have peace because "'for you who revere my name, the sun of righteousness will rise with healing in its wings. And you will go out and leap like calves released from the stall. Then you will trample down the wicked; they will be ashes under the soles of your feet on the day when I do these things,' says the LORD Almighty" (Malachi 4:2-3).

So Deborah's song points us to Jesus, who is spoken of in the Gospel in the same "rising sun" imagery: ". . . because of the tender mercy of our God, by which the rising sun will come to us from heaven to shine on those living in darkness and in the shadow of death, to guide our feet into the path of peace" (Luke 1:78-79).

The church's effectiveness in discipling God's people and in being salt and light in the culture will be in direct proportion to the quality of village life in the church. Village life is much more than fellowship dinners.

## VILLAGE LIFE NECESSITATES RADICAL OBEDIENCE

Penny Pappas understands this. This villager began a formal teaching ministry in her village when she was only fifteen. In the tiny kitchen of a country church, cluttered with porcelain coffeepots and empty vases, she fashioned a classroom complete with bulletin boards, handwork displays, and a sandbox depiction of the tabernacle. Over the years she taught in Christian day schools, youth groups, nursery, junior and primary departments of Sunday school, Bible conferences, Pioneer Clubs, women's home Bible studies, and in training seminars for other teachers. Finally the time came when she was ready to retire, or so she thought. This story is best told in Penny's own words.

> I had just turned sixty-five. Now I was old. Now it was time to sit back, warm the pews, and let the young people do the job. I would be there, however, to criticize. That was my retirement plan.
>
> But it wasn't God's plan, and it wasn't the plan of the elders and Sunday school superintendent. He approached me one Sunday. "Penny," he began, "we need a teacher in the

senior high class. And we've decided that all these younger people aren't cutting it. We need someone more mature to work with them."

"Sure," I responded scornfully, "someone big and old, but not me."

Taken aback the poor man said, "Will you at least pray about it?"

"No," I answered stubbornly, "I will not. Then I'll come back and blame my decision on the Lord. I have done my time. I really want a rest."

But that group of young people, challenging as they were, would not leave my mind: Heather, Susan, Sarah, Rob,* Laurie, Drew, Tim, Matt, Luke, Brooke, Steve, Todd, Amy, Rhonda, Chris. Some had been in my class when they were juniors. I knew their potential, and God was filling my heart with love for them and a real longing to share His Word with them. He was calling me to teach them.

"This old dog will just have to learn new tricks," I muttered as I contemplated the challenge of those unruly rascals who were so gifted mentally, artistically, and spiritually. I was truly no match for them, but experience told me that God had never, ever failed to equip me for a work He had called me to do.

And He did not fail me. Those youngsters still bring joy to my heart as I remember their hearty response to God's Word, their enthusiastic participation in class service projects, their growth in grace, and the deep love we shared for one another.[7]

---

*This is Rob Patete, who wrote the story about Penny at the beginning of this chapter.

Village life thrived in that class because this villager was willing to pay the price for village life. She was willing to leave her place of comfort and to forge ahead in obedience to the King of the village.

## POSTSCRIPT ON JUDGES

Now return to Judges 4 and 5. Not everyone in that community was willing to pay the price for village life. They heard the call, but warfare was too radical for them.

> *In the districts of Reuben there was much searching of heart. Why did you stay among the campfires to hear the whistling for the flocks?. . .*
>
> *Gilead stayed beyond the Jordan. . . .*
>
> *And Dan, why did he linger by the ships?*
>
> *Asher remained on the coast and stayed in his coves. . . .*
>
> *"Curse Meroz," said the angel of the LORD. "Curse its people bitterly, because they did not come to help the LORD, to help the LORD against the mighty."*
> —Judges 5:15-23

It is always that way. There are villagers who boldly take God at His Word and are "like the sun when it rises in its strength," and there are those who whistle for their flocks, stay in safe places beyond the Jordan, linger by their ships or in their coves, and receive a curse instead of a blessing. God's plan is not hindered in the least because of them. The tragedy is that they miss the celebration.

## TAKE-AWAY POINT

Villagers in the covenant village must rise above a needs-based theology that intensifies individualism. Their goal and their rallying point must be the honor of the King of the village. Anything less is destructive to village life. It is also destructive to personal peace. If our comfort zones put us on the periphery of village life, they cease to be comfort zones. We will find ourselves in positions of vulnerability to our own sin. Disobedience brings covenant curses. Obedience brings covenant blessings.

"Curse its people bitterly, because they did not come to help the LORD, to help the LORD against the mighty. . ." (Judges 5:23). "Then the land had peace forty years" (Judges 5:31). The village had peace, but some of the villagers experienced bitterness because they were content to sit on the sidelines.

Valiant villagers will labor with all their energy to "present everyone perfect in Christ" for the sake of Christ's Crown and Covenant.

---

∾

*Question:* What are some distinguishing characteristics of the covenant villagers and village?

*Answer:* The village teachers are characterized by a desire to share "not only the gospel of God but our lives as well" (1 Thessalonians 2:8). They know that they and their students need to strive against their inclination to self-centeredness and to grow in wisdom, maturity, and favor with God and man. The village is a safe, peaceful place where God's people become "like the sun when it rises in its strength" (Judges 5:31) and then go forth to be salt and light in the culture for the glory of Christ's Crown and Covenant.

---

BECOMING A COVENANT-KEEPER

1. Think about the influence of Lois, Eunice, and Paul in the life of Timothy. Have you had teachers who made such an imprint on your life? Make a list of the things they did. Are you doing these things for someone else?

2.  Read the teacher traits again and pray that these traits will be evident in your life. Write out one thought you have about each of the traits.

3.  Read Judges 4 and 5. What are some characteristics of village life in your church? What are you doing to make your village a safe place for other villagers? List some things your family or your class can do to promote village life.

CHRISTIAN EDUCATION IDEA

Recruiting, training, and retaining teachers is a primary responsibility of a Christian education committee. Careful consideration should be given to this task. You can have inadequate facilities and curriculum, and a good teacher, and students will be blessed. The reverse is also true.

*Recruiting Teachers*

The CE committee, or whoever is recruiting, should spend much time in prayer before asking anyone to take a teaching position. There should be a written job description that includes the doctrinal standards of the church, the purpose of the program, expectations of the teacher, length of time the person is being asked to teach, curriculum materials to be used, who the teacher reports to, training or other support that will be given, and any other needed information.

When approaching someone to teach, set aside a time when you will not be hurried. Tell the person that your committee has prayed and would like him or her to consider the position. Give the prospect a copy of the written job description and ask him or her to pray for a week before answering. Determine the time when you will call back to get an answer. Assure the prospect that the committee will also be praying during this time. Another approach is to send a letter with the job description and set a time when you will call for an answer.

## Training Teachers

Teacher training should equip teachers for the task. This training should include the overall vision for the church and for its CE program, as well as all of the issues covered in this book. In addition, there should be age-specific training or resources, possibly having someone with an education background do a segment on age characteristics.

Teachers should be challenged to have a purpose. Encourage each teacher to prayerfully set a "group goal" for his or her class by choosing at least one thing to accomplish. For example: the kindergarten class will learn to pray for one another; the senior highs will demonstrate a deeper understanding of the covenant community by becoming involved in ministries to younger children and to the elderly; the "Forty-Something" class will understand the compassion implications of the covenant and become involved in a ministry to the poor.

When teachers have this sense of purpose, their lessons should teach toward this goal. As they prepare each lesson, they can look at the lesson objectives in the curriculum and adapt these to their particular students and to their overall goal for the students. Training should emphasize the fact that you are not teaching individual lessons. Each lesson should help to move students toward a deeper understanding and application of God's Word. Having specific long-range goals will help the teacher to stay focused.

Encourage teachers to remember continually that they are to help students develop a biblical worldview that determines how they think and how they act.

Also encourage teachers to set personal goals. What are they praying will happen in their own lives to help them become more mature in Christ as a result of this teaching experience?

## Retaining Teachers

Once teachers are recruited and trained, there must be ongoing encouragement and support. Someone should be responsible for "caring" for teachers. Some ways this can be done:

- Install teachers during a worship service.
- Pray for teachers during worship services.
- Occasionally have a student or parent give a testimony about the influence of a teacher.
- Hold teacher gatherings with training, sharing, and times of prayer. Make these times of fun and relationship-building so that community is cultivated among teaching staff.
- Frequently send written memos with words of appreciation and information to be sure teachers always feel "in the loop."
- Have a Teacher Appreciation Month when the entire congregation is encouraged to express their appreciation to current and former teachers.
- Give a Teacher Appreciation Banquet.
- Recruit a prayer partner for each teacher. This could even be a homebound member.
- Be sure teachers have needed supplies. A well-kept supply closet is essential.
- Make sure you have clear procedures for discipline so the teacher is not in doubt about what to do. Parents should also know the procedures so that the teacher is not put in an awkward situation.

# 9

*For Christ's Crown
and Covenant*

—
ℛ
—

# LIVING AND TEACHING
# COVENANTALLY

## A SUNDAY SCHOOL TEACHER

I did not have the privilege of growing up in a Christian home, but my parents were very moral people and wanted their children to be in church. Every week from the time I was in second grade, my mother faithfully took us to Sunday school although she did not attend herself. When my parents selected a church for us, they chose one that was next door to my grandmother's house. It was convenient for my mother to drop us off at the door and when Sunday school was over, we walked to my grandmother's. From my parents' perspective, it was a decision based on convenience. In God's sovereign providence, Trinity Presbyterian Church in Montgomery, Alabama, was known for its strong, biblically based teaching and excellent teachers.

I can still remember my first Sunday school class and the teacher who presented the flannelgraph lesson. I remember her warmth for her second grade girls and the enthusiasm with which she presented the lesson. It was the first time I had ever heard the name of Jesus.

In the fourth grade, my teacher was Mrs. Peggy Joseph. This lady has had a profound impact on my life. Her investment in me went far beyond the classroom. She encouraged me to participate with her in appropriate activities. I was able to attend Vacation Bible School and Good News Clubs because of her invitations. I graduated from her class but evidently not from her heart. In the years that followed, she continued to check up on me through classes and activities at church as well as through personal phone calls. In junior high I was able to attend many of the overnight retreats and camps, as well as the youth group meetings, because she called my mother to assure her that it would be good for me.

During my junior high years, I was invited to Mrs. Joseph's home many times for meals and just to "hang out" with her children. Since she has three sons, she affectionately called me her daughter. In their home I was aware of the differences in the way a Christian family lived. I observed immediate obedience to parents, prayer before meals, and family Bible reading. Because of their home and lifestyle, I determined at that time that I wanted a Christian home.

I received Christ as my Savior at a camp the summer before entering eighth grade. One of her sons told Mrs. Joseph of my commitment to the Lord. I remember the conversation she had with me as she told me the importance of prayer and Bible reading. Throughout my high school years, she continued to love and encourage me. She prayed for my parents and siblings, all of whom eventually came to faith in Christ.

After my graduation from high school, I attended a Christian college and received a degree in Christian education. My husband and I have nine children whom we homeschool. Many of the principles that I saw practiced in Mrs. Joseph's home are now being lived out in our home. I have a passion to teach my own children as well as children in the church.

After twenty years, I returned to my home church to give a presentation for Sunday school teachers. It was a time of introspection and reflection for me. Mrs. Joseph sat in the audience. In characteristic form, I received a letter from her the following week telling me that she had been blessed by my teaching.

Mrs. Joseph still teaches the fourth grade Sunday school class, and I am confident she continues to have a lifelong impact on the children God brings to her.

—Priscilla Stewart,
Montgomery, Alabama

# For Christ's Crown and Covenant

∾

Many years ago, when I taught kindergarten, the children called me "teacher." Every day I reminded them of my name. It took several weeks for some of them to remember. I'm sorry I bothered. Teacher ranks right up there with Mom and Dad.

Apparently Jesus liked it too. His disciples often called Him "teacher." After the ascension of Jesus, two of His students were arrested for preaching that He was alive. When Peter and John stood before the religious leaders, they were fearless in their witness. The reaction of the rulers, elders, and teachers of the law is telling: "When they saw the courage of Peter and John and realized that they were unschooled, ordinary men, they were astonished and they took note that these men had been with Jesus" (Acts 4:13).

The very thing that the religious leaders noted about Peter and John (they had been with Jesus) was Jesus' teaching strategy from the beginning. We read that when He called the disciples, "He appointed twelve—designating them apostles—that they might be with him and that he might send them out to preach" (Mark 3:14).

This is the way it works. The relationship (that they might be with Him) precedes the task (sent them out to preach). The relationship gives confidence for the task.

He appointed twelve that they might be *with Him*. Again we see the covenant promise: I will be your God, you will be my people, I will live among you. The gift of living in His presence, of being *with Him*, is the provision of the covenant of grace. It is His presence that distinguishes us from all the other people on the face of the earth (Exodus 33:16). It certainly distinguished Peter and John.

The religious leaders were astonished because Peter and John were unschooled, ordinary men. Jesus did not go after the best and the brightest. He took the base and the boring and made them into the best and the brightest. He took the fearful and made them fearless. He took the cowardly and made them confident. He even took a denier and made him into a defender. Uneducated, unsophisticated men were transformed into bold, confident apologists because they had been with Jesus.

When Peter and John stood before the religious leaders, they did not experience a surge of courageous self-confidence. They banked on their knowledge of and relationship with the King of Glory. Their unswerving confidence was in His covenant of grace and His sovereign ability to keep the covenant promise. It was Christ's Crown and Covenant that empowered and emboldened them.

Our teaching must confront our students with Christ's crown rights over them and His covenant of love to redeem them. This is the only thing that will transform them from the base and the boring to the best and the brightest who "shine like the brightness of the heavens . . . like the stars for ever and ever" (Daniel 12:3). This is the only thing that will encourage and empower them to go the distance so they can say with Paul, "I have fought the good fight, I have finished the race, I have kept the faith" (2 Timothy 4:7).

## FROM WORST TO FIRST

The 1991 Atlanta Braves baseball team became known as the "Miracle Braves" because they went from "worst to first." The 1990 Braves were last in their league. In 1991 they won the National League championship. A sports psychologist played a part in this success.

When pitcher John Smoltz was struggling, the psychologist videotaped him pitching a perfect fast ball, a perfect curve ball, a perfect you-name-it. Over and over, day after day, Smoltz watched the video. Then when he got into trouble on the mound, he "replayed" the video in his mind. Visualizing a perfect pitch helped him deliver.

Smoltz had the technique and the ability, but he needed the

confidence to believe he could throw a strike in a difficult situation. The problem was not *competence* but *confidence*. The psychologist provided the confidence-builder, and Smoltz went on to lead the Braves to the World Series.

A teacher of truth does more than impart information. He/she sees every student as "God's workmanship, created in Christ Jesus to do good works, which God prepared in advance for us to do" (Ephesians 2:10). This teacher does not just see what his students are. He sees what they can be in the power of grace. If our students are Christians, they are heirs of the covenant, so they are competent to do the good works God prepared in advance for them to do. They have the very Spirit of God living within them. Our task is to develop their confidence, not in self but in Christ.

We can learn something from the sports psychologist who provided the confidence-builder for John Smoltz. He repeatedly replayed a video. He showed Smoltz what the pitcher could be and do. We must repeatedly hold Christ's Crown and Covenant before our students. We must show them what they can be and do through Christ. We must play this message before them in every lesson and in the example of our lives, or they will drift into a performance-based obedience rather than a grace-empowered obedience. Obedience based on self-effort will strike out every time. It is the miracle of grace that transforms our students.

"And we, who with unveiled faces all reflect the Lord's glory, are being transformed into his likeness with ever-increasing glory, which comes from the Lord, who is the Spirit" (2 Corinthians 3:18). It is grace that empowers your students to ". . . throw off everything that hinders and the sin that so easily entangles, and . . . run with perseverance the race marked out for [them]" (Hebrews 12:1).

## FROM ORPHAN TO QUEEN

The Old Testament story of Esther, a young Jewish girl who became queen of Persia and was used of God to deliver her people from annihilation, is a stunning example of obedience. Her classic statement: "I will go to the king. . . . And if I perish, I perish" (Esther 4:16), has inspired people throughout the ages. I think, however, that we are often so captivated with Esther that we miss the rest of the story.

This is a story of sovereign grace. It is a story of a teacher of grace who confronted his student with the crown rights of Jehovah and with His covenant of grace to redeem His people.

Esther's cousin Mordecai was a master teacher. When Esther became queen of Persia, and wicked Haman persuaded her husband to issue an edict that all Jews were to be killed, Mordecai appealed to her to be the advocate for her people before the king. Mordecai loved Esther. Asking her to take such a risk must have been a difficult decision. But she was in the most strategic position to be used in this crisis, and Mordecai must have recognized this as God's providential plan.

Consider Mordecai's strategy in appealing to Esther.

First, his appeal was not given in a vacuum. It was presented in the context of a caring relationship. His entry into Esther's life did not occur suddenly when the Jewish people were threatened. Instead "Mordecai had taken her as his own daughter when her father and mother died" (Esther 2:7). He accepted this little orphaned girl, loved her as his own daughter, and made a significant investment in her life.

Second, when Esther was taken into the king's harem, Mordecai did not abandon her. "Every day he walked back and forth near the courtyard of the harem to find out how Esther was and what was happening to her" (Esther 2:11).

Third, while Esther lived in his home, Mordecai faithfully instructed her. Esther trusted this instruction and put it into practice when she was taken into the king's harem. "Esther had kept secret her family background and nationality just as Mordecai had told her to do, for she continued to follow Mordecai's instructions as she had done when he was bringing her up" (Esther 2:20).

There was neither a relationship vacuum nor an information vacuum. He taught the content of the covenant in the context of covenant love.

When the crisis came, and Mordecai appealed to Esther, she understandably hesitated. The stakes were high. Mordecai persisted. His challenge reveals his covenantal perspective. "Do not think that because you are in the king's house you alone of all the Jews will escape. For if you remain silent at this time, relief and deliverance for the Jews will arise from another place, but you and your father's family will perish. And who knows but that you have come to royal position for such a time as this?" (Esther 4:13-14).

It is often assumed that the power of his challenge is in the words, "And who knows but that you have come to royal position for such a time as this?" But I believe the confidence-builder is in the sentence that preceded that magnificent conclusion: "For if you remain silent at this time, relief and deliverance for the Jews *will arise* from another place. . . ."

Deliverance *will* arise—this is the tree (the redemptive message). All the other people and events are the acorns (see chapter 3). This is not about Esther. This is about the sovereign King keeping His promise to redeem the heirs of the covenant.

Deliverance *will* arise—with or without Esther.

How could Mordecai be so sure?

How could the apostle Paul make the same claim when, from prison awaiting execution, he wrote to Timothy, "The Lord *will* rescue me from every evil attack and *will* bring me safely to his heavenly kingdom"? (2 Timothy 4:18)

How could they be so confident?

Because they knew about the smoking firepot.

FROM BELIEF TO CONFIDENCE

Genesis 15 is the keynote address on confidence to fight the good fight, finish the race, and keep the faith.

It had been years since God first appeared to Abraham and promised an heir. Abraham was still childless. A child was an essential element of the covenant promise. Abraham and Sarah were dead as far as their physical ability to have a child, so Abraham assumed that the son of his servant would receive the inheritance. God again spoke to Abraham and gave him an incredible object lesson. He told him to go out and look at the stars. "Then the word of the LORD came to him: 'This man will not be your heir, but a son coming from your own body will be your heir.' He took him outside and said, 'Look up at the heavens and count the stars—if indeed you can count them.' Then he said to him, 'So shall your offspring be.' Abram believed the LORD, and he credited it to him as righteousness" (Genesis 15:4-6).

Abraham believed despite the human impossibility, but he asked the question that Esther must have asked deep in her heart. Mordecai and Paul must have asked the question. It is the question we all ask. "Abram said, 'O Sovereign LORD, how can I know that I will gain possession of it?'" (Genesis 15:8).

I believe, but how can I *know*? It is God's answer that moved Abraham from belief to strong confidence. This confidence later was demonstrated when he obeyed God's command, took the promised child to lay him on the altar, and answered the child's question about where they would get the lamb for the offering with the words, "God himself *will* provide . . ." (Genesis 22:8).

It is God's answer to this question that gave Mordecai the confidence to say, "Relief and deliverance for the Jews *will arise* . . ."

It is God's answer to this question that gave Paul the confidence to say, "The Lord *will* rescue me from every evil attack and *will* bring me safely to his heavenly kingdom" (2 Timothy 4:18).

It is God's answer to this question that will give us and our students the confidence to fight the good fight, finish the race, and keep the faith.

> So the LORD said to [Abraham], "Bring me a heifer, a goat and a ram, each three years old, along with a dove and a young pigeon."
>
> Abram brought all these to him, cut them in two and arranged the halves opposite each other. . . .

*As the sun was setting, Abram fell into a deep sleep, and a
thick and dreadful darkness came over him. . . . When the sun
had set and darkness had fallen, a smoking firepot with a blazing torch appeared and passed between the pieces.*

*On that day the LORD made a covenant with Abram and
said, "To your descendants I give this land, from the river of
Egypt to the great river, the Euphrates. . . ."*

*Genesis 15:9ff.*

The smoking firepot and the blazing torch are symbols of God's
presence. "By passing between the torn animals (signifying the
punishment due those who break the covenant), God invokes a
self-maledictory oath or curse upon Himself should He fail to keep
His covenant. Because He can swear by no higher authority, God
swears by Himself to keep the covenantal terms."[1]

Passing between sacrificed animals was a common ritual in
that culture. It guaranteed that if the oath-taker broke his word, he
could be torn apart like the animals. In this remarkable passage, the
King of Glory assures us that if He breaks His covenant promise,
He will destroy Himself.

Relief and deliverance *will* arise; the Lord *will* rescue us and
bring us to His heavenly kingdom, because He promised. He is
oath-bound. If He fails to keep His promise, He will tear Himself
apart. Our confidence has nothing to do with ourselves. It has
everything to do with God.

Caution: We must not confine our understanding of relief and
deliverance to this earthly realm or to our outward circumstances.

BACK TO PERSIA

When the threat of annihilation came, Mordecai could say with
confident assurance that deliverance would come. Mordecai spoke
words that reminded Esther to reach back to what he had taught
her about the character and promises of Jehovah. Notice the wisdom of his appeal.

He did not devastate Esther by rebuking her when she faltered: "If you were really committed, you would not hesitate to assume this responsibility."

Neither did he use guilt: "I've done so much for you—you owe me."

Nor did he build up a false confidence by focusing on her own abilities, accomplishments, or circumstances: "Esther, you are so successful and loved. You can do it!"

Instead, he reminded her of her identity as a child of the covenant.

> *"Do not think that because you are in the king's house you alone of all the Jews will escape."*

He reminded her of God's faithfulness to His covenant people.

> *"For if you remain silent at this time, relief and deliverance for the Jews will arise from another place. . . ."*

He confronted her with the dreadful consequences of being a covenant-breaker.

> *". . .but you and your father's family will perish."*

He reminded her of God's providence in her life and that this just may be the good work that God prepared in advance for her to do.

> *"And who knows but that you have come to royal position for such a time as this?"*
>
> —*Esther 4:13-14*

The good works that our students were created and redeemed to do are impossible apart from grace. Mordecai made no pretense that this was an achievable act of obedience. He wisely realized that the overwhelming importance and urgency of this situation was beyond Esther's internal resources. He focused her on the person and promises of God. Esther's confidence in God swelled and her immediate response was to act covenantally.

> *Then Esther sent this reply to Mordecai: "Go, gather together all the Jews who are in Susa, and fast for me. Do not eat or drink for three days, night or day. I and my maids will fast as you do. When this is done, I will go to the king, even though it is against the law. And if I perish, I perish."*
> —Esther 4:15-16

He had taught her well. She did not act independently. She remembered that she was part of the covenant community. She requested their support as she made preparations to go to the king on their behalf.

"If I perish, I perish," are not words of noble resignation. They are words of confident hope in, and abandonment to, Christ's Crown and Covenant. If she perishes in this life, she will live in eternity. Whatever God does is good because He is good.

Events took an extraordinary twist. The king gave wicked Haman's estate to Esther and then said to Esther and Mordecai:

> *"Now write another decree in the king's name in behalf of the Jews as seems best to you, and seal it with the king's signet ring." . . . Mordecai left the king's presence wearing royal garments of blue and white, a large crown of gold and a purple robe of fine linen. . . . Mordecai was prominent in the palace; his reputation spread throughout the provinces, and he became more and more powerful.*
> —Esther 8:8, 15; 9:4

This is a crisis of a different sort. This is where we most often falter. In many ways, this is where Mordecai taught his greatest lesson. It is one thing to be dependent on God's grace when we are in danger. It is another thing to cling to grace when we are successful.

Power and prestige did not deflect Mordecai. Glamour and glitz did not sway him. He did not seek acclaim for himself. He did not bask in the glory. He quickly made provision for the people to remember that it was God's covenant faithfulness that delivered them and gave them rest and relief from their enemies.

*Mordecai recorded these events, and he sent letters to all the Jews throughout the provinces of King Xerxes, near and far, to have them celebrate annually the fourteenth and fifteenth days of the month of Adar as the time when the Jews got relief from their enemies, and as the month when their sorrow was turned into joy and their mourning into a day of celebration. He wrote them to observe the days as days of feasting and joy and giving presents of food to one another and gifts to the poor. . . . (Therefore these days were called Purim, from the word* pur.) *Because of everything written in this letter and because of what they had seen and what had happened to them, the Jews took it upon themselves to establish the custom that they and their descendants and all who join them should without fail observe these two days every year, in the way prescribed and at the time appointed. These days should be remembered and observed in every generation by every family, and in every province and in every city. And these days of Purim should never cease to be celebrated by the Jews, nor should the memory of them die out among their descendants.*

*So Queen Esther . . . along with Mordecai . . . wrote with full authority. . . . And Mordecai sent letters to all the Jews in the 127 provinces of the kingdom of Xerxes—words of good will and assurance—to establish these days of Purim . . . as Mordecai the Jew and Queen Esther had decreed for them, and as they had established for themselves and their descendants in regard to their times of fasting and lamentation.*

*—Esther 9:20-31*

Royal robes and palaces of prominence are spiritual minefields. Pride, independence, self-promotion, and lust for more power and prominence threaten to explode in our souls. We must walk carefully and prayerfully if God puts us in this position. We must also remember that He put us there and He can take us out at any moment. We are not there because we deserve it. We are there to serve His purposes. Apparently Mordecai remembered, and he involved his young student in the process of teaching the people that it was God who had delivered them and God who should be praised.

Mordecai was indeed a covenantal teacher. When Esther came into his home, he had no clue that she would play a vital role in Jewish history, but perhaps he did recognize the situation as an opportunity from God to make an investment in a child. Rather than viewing Esther as an intrusion and a burden, perhaps he had a mental picture of her being used to serve God. He taught her of her heritage and the promises God had made to His people. Perhaps he saw her as God's workmanship, created for a specific purpose in God's sovereign plan. Perhaps he helped her to visualize herself responding to Jehovah's faithfulness in obedience regardless of the circumstance. Then, when the crisis came, she replayed the video and delivered the strike. She fought the good fight; she kept the faith.

Teachers need to have a vision of their students confidently and boldly serving the Lord God. We need to challenge our students to lives of servanthood, but we must not issue the challenge in a vacuum. We must be willing to make the investment, to give faithful instruction, to nurture, and then to sound a clarion call to obedience. But we must never talk of obedience apart from God's grace that enables us to obey. The King calls us to be with Him (the covenant of grace), and then He sends us forth to do the good works He prepared in advance for us to do.

Are there Mordecais today who will make long-term investments in the lives of students? What can possibly motivate us to go the distance and to make sacrificial investments in our students?

## LONG-DISTANCE TEACHERS

Years ago I hit a brick wall in my desire to invest in the lives of students. I was tired. They were not responsive. I had serious questions about the wisdom of pouring myself into people who were indifferent. I went to the Word before I gave up completely. This is what I learned.

Just a few hours before His crucifixion, Jesus washed the disciples' feet (John 13). After the Resurrection, He cooked breakfast for them. The Teacher/King served His students, even the one who denied Him. In fact, He took extra care to reach out to Peter.

> *When they had finished eating, Jesus said to Simon Peter, "Simon son of John, do you truly love me more than these?" "Yes, Lord," he said, "you know that I love you." Jesus said, "Feed my lambs."*
>
> *Again Jesus said, "Simon son of John, do you truly love me?" He answered, "Yes, Lord, you know that I love you." Jesus said, "Take care of my sheep."*
>
> *The third time he said to him, "Simon son of John, do you love me?" Peter was hurt because Jesus asked him the third time, "Do you love me?" He said, "Lord, you know all things; you know that I love you." Jesus said, "Feed my sheep."*
>
> —John 21:15-17

We demonstrate our love for Jesus by feeding and taking care of His sheep. Sometimes the sheep are dirty, stubborn, resistant, and rebellious. We don't feed them because they are cute and cuddly. We feed them because we love Jesus. This is our calling.

But sometimes my love for Jesus is simply not strong enough to keep me going. It pains me to write this, but it is true. The calling to feed the sheep because of my love for Jesus drives me to my need for grace. Paul must have felt this when he defined the motivating force in his life: "For Christ's love compels us, because we are convinced that one died for all, and therefore all died" (2 Corinthians 5:14).

There is nothing in us or in our students that will compel us to cross the finish line. We must continually go to the cross and drink deeply of grace. We must daily preach the Gospel to ourselves. We must meditate on the amazing undeserved love of Jesus for sinners, of whom I am chief. When the smoking firepot passed through the torn animals, God swore by Himself to meet the covenantal terms. He kept those terms when Jesus hung on the cross. We cannot begin to fathom the agony of the Father and the Son as they were torn asunder from each other because the Son was covered with our sin. But the Resurrection is proof that the payment was sufficient. The terms were met. Our redemption is secure. We live in His presence.

> *Therefore, since we have a great high priest who has gone through the heavens, Jesus the Son of God, let us hold firmly to the faith we profess. For we do not have a high priest who is unable to sympathize with our weaknesses, but we have one who has been tempted in every way, just as we are—yet was without sin. Let us then approach the throne of grace with confidence, so that we may receive mercy and find grace to help us in our time of need.*
> —Hebrews 4:14-16

Christ's Crown and Covenant compel us to care for His lambs, and we can go confidently to His throne of grace to find grace to do so.

## TEACH MY CHILDREN

In 1907 a young dying mother had one desire for her children. She traveled to Columbus, Mississippi, by train with her infant and two toddlers. The train was met by Mrs. William Frierson, head matron and wife of the superintendent of Palmer Home for Children. Mrs. Frierson wrote that when she saw the frail form of the dying woman, carrying her crying infant while two toddlers tugged at her dress, "My heart leaped into my throat, and for a moment I seemed ready to yield to a flood of tears." The young mother's parting words to Mrs. Frierson are indelibly etched in the Palmer consciousness: "Teach my children to meet me in heaven."

Dr. Ed Waldron, director of Palmer Home for Children, writes:

> Those words have become Palmer's watchwords, our rallying call to mission. And it is, as you think about it, a most comprehensive charge—teach my children to live, teach them to die, teach them to meet the Lord.
>
> Yet for all its gripping poignancy, most would think that Palmer's work and worth for these children was completed some 80 or so years ago. So you can imagine my complete surprise when we received a letter from the daughter-in-law of one of those three children!
>
> The little toddler tugging at her mother's dress is now a 95-year-old woman confined to a New Jersey nursing home. But her daughter-in-law wrote to thank us for the solid Christian upbringing her mother-in-law had received at Palmer Home. She couldn't begin to tell us, she said, of the impact of that godly woman in her life, in her husband's life, in their children's lives, and now in the lives of their grandchildren. . . . A strategic investment in a young life at a point of desperate need has changed a child for good . . . changed a marriage . . . indeed, changed a family's history for now four generations.[2]

Many have fought the good fight and kept the faith because a young mother knew that the only thing that mattered was for someone to teach her children to meet her in heaven, and there were people who were willing to teach them about the King of Glory who entered into a covenant of grace to save a people to live with Him for eternity.

Dr. Edmund P. Clowney penned a hymn that surely expresses the thoughts this young mother and Mrs. Frierson must have had. Perhaps it also expresses the thoughts Mordecai had when he received the little orphaned girl into his home.

*In your arms, Lord Jesus Christ, children have a place;*
*brought to you to feel your touch, Lord, bless them with your*
*grace.*

*Savior, on these little ones place your Father's claim;*
*seal them as his children, Jesus, give to them your name.*

*Wash them at the fountain, Lord, opened for our sin;*
*we baptize with water's symbol; yours to cleanse within.*

*Yours they are, our heritage, granted in your love;*
*children of your promise, Savior, send your Spirit's dove.*

*Teach us, Lord, to teach your child; guide us as we guide.*
*Lead this little one to know you, joyful at your side.*[3]

TAKE-AWAY POINT

Confidence to fight the good fight, finish the race, and keep the
faith is based upon the character and promise of God.

> *When God made his promise to Abraham, since there was no*
> *one greater for him to swear by, he swore by himself, saying,*
> *"I will surely bless you and give you many descendants."*
> *. . . Because God wanted to make the unchanging nature of*
> *his purpose very clear to the heirs of what was promised, he*
> *confirmed it with an oath.*
> *God did this so that . . . we who have fled to take hold of the*
> *hope offered to us may be greatly encouraged. We have this*
> *hope as an anchor for the soul, firm and secure.*
>                                    —Hebrews 6:13-19

Toward the end of the fourth century B.C., the Jewish nation
was in jeopardy. Mordecai reminded his student of God's character and promise. Esther took hold of the hope, it became the anchor
for her soul, and she confidently stepped forward and served her

God by being the advocate for His people before the king. The deliverance is celebrated to this day in the Jewish community in the festival of Purim.

Now, nearing the end of the twentieth century, the church is under attack. Will our students step forward with confidence to gather under the banner of Christ's Crown and Covenant that future generations may celebrate God's deliverance?

Are there teachers who will prepare the heirs of the covenant for such a time as this?

We must—for Christ's Crown and Covenant.

*Question:* Why do we live and teach covenantally?

*Answer:* Because of the crown rights of King Jesus over all creation and because of His covenant of grace to purchase us for Himself.

*Question:* How do we develop confident students who will fight the good fight, finish the race, and keep the faith?

*Answer:* By pointing them to God's faithfulness to His covenant promise and by teaching them to draw on His grace to obey His commands. We must teach them to be with Him—to live in His presence—that they might do the good works He created them to do.

BECOMING A COVENANT-KEEPER

1.  Read Hebrews 10:19-25.
    *   Why do we have confidence to enter the Most Holy Place?
    *   Write a statement of what it means to you personally that you can go to the very throne of God—into His presence—with confidence.

- According to verses 23-25, what are our covenant responsibilities because of the covenant privilege of confident access to God's presence?

2. Read Hebrews 11 and meditate on the confidence these heroes of faith had in God's promise.

3. Read Hebrews 12:1-3. What sins entangle you and slow your race? What sins hinder your ability to encourage others to love and good deeds? Fix your spiritual eyes on Jesus. Go confidently to His throne of grace and find grace to repent. Then go forth in the power of grace to touch others with grace and mercy.

4. What did you learn from Mordecai's example that will help you as you teach your children, grandchildren, students?

5. Look back over each chapter and list several things you have learned from this study. What difference is this knowledge making in your life?

CHRISTIAN EDUCATION IDEA

This potpourri of ideas is reprinted from several issues of the *Bulletin Supplement*, a publication of the Christian Education and Publications Committee of the Presbyterian Church in America.

*Operation Child to Child:* During the month of December, the children of Mitchell Road Presbyterian Church in Greenville, South Carolina, were invited to experience the joy of giving. A child in a Greenville hospital with an unhappy family situation was assigned to each Sunday school class. The children of the church were told only the first initial of the child's name, age, favorite color, and clothing sizes. The children brought Christmas gifts of clothing and Bibles for the hospitalized children.

*Christmas Night Special:* Members of Calvary Presbyterian Church in Willow Grove, Pennsylvania, went door to door on Christmas evening giving loaves of cranberry bread, wishing their unchurched neighbors merry Christmas, and inviting them to visit the church. Included with each loaf was a copy of the Gospel of John and information about the church.

*Baby Bottle Banks:* Members of Evangelical Presbyterian Church of Baltimore, Maryland, are given baby bottles for families to use as banks to collect their loose change and give to a crisis pregnancy center.

*Bring Them In:* Trinity Presbyterian Church in Charlottesville, Virginia, provides transportation to church for disabled residents in their area. Arrangements are made with a local company for the use of vans equipped with hydraulic lifts. Members of the church volunteer for the training course and driving test. Volunteers work in teams of two to bring wheelchair-bound men and women to worship.

*College Boxes and Christmas Ornaments:* Twice each year members of Midway Presbyterian Church in Powder Springs, Georgia, mail a "care" box to their college students. The project reminds the students that they are missed, loved, and remembered. Included are candy, gum, pencils, post-it notes, microwave popcorn, and other small items. The church's children are celebrated with a "Covenant Children's Christmas Tree." Each year pictures are collected of all the children, and tree ornaments are designed and made by the women in the church. These are used on the Christmas tree in the fellowship hall. After Christmas the parents take the ornaments to use in future years on their own trees.

*Outreach to Neighbors:* A free car wash—no strings attached—is offered to the residents living in the apartments and neighborhood surrounding Lakemont Presbyterian Church in Augusta, Georgia. The purpose is to connect with people and to invite them to worship services and other church functions. An added blessing to church members comes from working together to reach out and serve.

*Bassinet Project:* The women's Sunday school class at Bethel Presbyterian Church in Clover, South Carolina, has a bassinet in the classroom for members to bring baby clothes, diapers, blankets, and other items needed by the local crisis pregnancy center.

*Church Bulletin in Braille:* At Green Lake Presbyterian Church in

Seattle, Washington, the bulletin is translated into Braille for the sight-impaired.

*Kid Art:* At Tyrone Covenant Presbyterian Church in Fenton, Michigan, seven- to nine-year-old children submit pictures depicting a Bible story. These are used as bulletin covers. On the Sunday when a child's picture is used, the child goes to the pulpit and tells the story illustrated by the picture.

*Singles Ministry:* For twenty years the Seekers and the Koinonia Sunday school classes prayed for a singles ministry at First Presbyterian Church in Augusta, Georgia. When a class for singles was finally started, it flourished and grew until a second class was begun. In thanksgiving for the answered prayers, the Seekers and Koinonias hosted the singles for lunch after the Sunday morning service. The event is now an annual affair.

*Medical Professionals for Christ:* A nine-hour seminar for doctors and dentists was jointly sponsored by Park Cities Presbyterian Church in Dallas, Texas, and Medical Professionals for Christ. The seminar sought to answer the questions: "How can a busy doctor or dentist with a waiting room full of patients take time to share his or her faith?" The professionals, their spouses, and staff discussed how to influence the spiritual health of their patients "by sharing spiritual truth in just twenty seconds!" The church also hosted a seminar by Law Professionals for Christ and the Rutherford Institute. The seminar helped those attending understand the religious liberties they possess and gave suggestions for practicing their faith in school, at work, and in their families.

*Ministry to Foreign Students:* Students from all over the world attending the University of Delaware are invited to participate in worship services and other activities at Evangelical Presbyterian Church in Newark, Delaware. Church members transport the students to services and other functions. EPC families "host" foreign students by contacting them at least once a month to see how they are doing, check on their needs, and offer assistance.

*Community Ministries:* Faith Presbyterian Church in Paris, Texas, has a strong commitment to reach out to the local community. A free medical clinic operated by volunteer professionals provides health services, food is collected for the poor, an outreach to recently released prisoners meets on Sunday afternoons, and members make contacts with a small group of Muslims in the community.

*Verse of the Month:* The entire congregation at New Life Presbyterian Church in Aliquippa, Pennsylvania, is challenged to participate in a program to memorize a verse of Scripture every month. The verse to be memorized is published in the Sunday morning bulletin and emphasized by the pastor. Families are asked to post the verse in a convenient place in the home where the entire family can learn it together.

*Friends of David:* There is no way to know how David will respond or what he might do. He may remove his shoes or suddenly leap up and remove all the contents from a table, or he may surprise his friends with his smile and a quiet song. David is a special child. His friends at Oakwood Presbyterian Church in State College, Pennsylvania, take turns sitting with him on Sunday mornings to provide a time for his parents to attend worship. His friends consider it a privilege to share this time with David. The church has a "Disability Awareness Sunday" when members are encouraged to bring friends or family members with disabilities. Caregivers are encouraged and provided help in ministering to those with disabilities.

# NOTES

## FOREWORD

1. Cornelius Van Til, *Foundations for Christian Education* (Phillipsburg, N.J.: Presbyterian and Reformed Publishers, 1990), 116.

## 1
## THE CONTENT OF THE COVENANT

1. John Howie, *The Scots Worthies*, rev. W. H. Carslaw (Edinburgh: The Banner of Truth Trust, 1870, reprinted 1995), 11-12.
2. Ibid., 16.
3. Ibid., 124-125.
4. Fitzroy MacLean, *Scotland: A Concise History* (London: Thames and Hudson, 1995), 116.
5. Howie, *Scots Worthies*, 492-493.
6. *The Westminster Confession of Faith*, VII, 1 (Atlanta: The Committee for Christian Education & Publications, 1990), 24.
7. O. Palmer Robertson, *The Christ of the Covenants* (Phillipsburg, N.J.: Presbyterian and Reformed Publishers, 1980), 3-4.
8. S. G. DeGraaf, *Promise and Deliverance*, vol. 1 (Ontario: Paideia Press, 1977), 21.
9. Ibid., "The Christ of the Covenants," 4.
10. Ibid., "Promise and Deliverance," 24.

## 2
## THE CONTEXT OF THE COVENANT

1. Muriel Larson, "Four Teachers, Four Lives," in *Success: Christian Education Today*, ed. Edith Quinlan (Denver, Colo.: An Accent Publication, vol. 37 no. 2 (Spring 1985), 22.
2. Ibid., 21.
3. *The Westminster Shorter Catechism*, Q. 34 (Atlanta: PCA Committee for Christian Education & Publications, 1990).

4.  Ibid., *The Westminster Confession of Faith*, chapter XII, 42-43.

5.  Reformed University Ministries, a division of the Mission to North America Committee of the Presbyterian Church in America, December 1996 Newsletter.

6.  George Grant, *The Patriot's Handbook* (Elkton, Md.: Highland Books, 1996), 22.

7.  Ibid., 27.

8.  *The Westminster Confession of Faith*, chapter XXVI, 1-2.

3
## THE BOOK OF THE COVENANT

1.  Lewis Berkhof, *Systematic Theology* (Grand Rapids, Mich.: Eerdmans, 1977), 558-559.

2.  John Calvin, *Institutes of the Christian Religion*, vol. 2, ed. John T. McNeill (Philadelphia: Westminster Press, 1960), 1024.

3.  Bryan Chapell, *Christ-Centered Preaching* (Grand Rapids, Mich.: Baker Books, 1994), 270

4.  "'This Is My Name': God's Self-disclosure," *New Geneva Study Bible*, R. C. Sproul, ed. (Nashville: Thomas Nelson, 1995), 98.

5.  S. G. DeGraaf, *Promise and Deliverance*, vol. 1 (Ontario: Paideia Press, 1977), 20.

6.  Richard J. Mouw, *Uncommon Decency* (Downers Grove, Ill.: InterVarsity Press, 1992), 146.

7.  An excellent example of this approach is *Memory Work Notebook*, by Paul G. Settle, published by Great Commission Publications. It may be ordered by calling 1-800-283-1357.

4
## HOME AND CHURCH

1.  J. C. Ryle, *The Duties of Parents* (Conrad, Mont.: Triangle Press, 1993), 14-15, first printed by Wm. Hunt & Co., 1888.

2.  *Tabletalk*, March 1996, 58-59.

3.  J. C. Ryle, *A Call to Prayer, An Urgent Plea to Enter into the Secret Place* (Laurel, Miss.: Audubon Press, 1996), 34-35.

4.  Charles Hodge, *Systematic Theology*, vol. 3 (Grand Rapids, Mich.: Eerdmans, 1991), 555.

5.  Elisabeth Elliot, *A Chance to Die* (Old Tappan, N.J.: Fleming H. Revell, 1987), 187.

6. Ibid., p. 199.

7. Amy Carmichael, "For Our Children," in *Toward Jerusalem* (Ft. Washington, Penn.: Christian Literature Crusade, 1936) p. 106. Used by permission of the Dohnavur Fellowship.


5
A COVENANTAL STRATEGY FOR CHURCH GROWTH

1. Robert Rayburn, "The Doctrines of Covenant Children, Covenant Nurture, and Covenant Succession," *Presbyterian: Covenant Seminary Review*, vol. 22, no. 2 (Fall 1996), 76-108.

2. From a telephone interview with Bill Armes.

3. Augustine, *Confessions*, introduction.

4. Ibid., p. 13.

5. Ibid., p. 16.

6. Ibid., p. 22.

7. Ibid., p. 25.

8. Ibid., p. 58.

9. Alexander Whyte, *The Holy War*, Bunyan Characters, Third Series (London: Oliphant Anderson and Ferrier, 1902), 289-290.


6
TEACHING COVENANTALLY

1. *The Westminster Shorter Catechism, The Westminster Confession of Faith*, I.2. (Atlanta: PCA Committee for Christian Education & Publications, 1990).

2. George Grant, "Classical and Covenantal," in *Covenanter*, vol. 1, no. 1 (Spring 1997) (Franklin, Tenn.: Covenant Classical School Association).

3. R. Laird Harris, Gleason L. Archer, Jr., Bruce K. Waltke, *Theological Wordbook of the Old Testament*, vol. 1 (Chicago: Moody Press, 1980), 367.


7
A STRATEGY FOR CHRISTIAN EDUCATION

1. Allen Curry, "Christian Education: A Blue Chip Ministry," in *Equip* (Jan/Feb 1996), p. 8 (Atlanta, Ga.: PCA Committee for Christian Education & Publications).

2. Ibid.

3. Allen Curry, "Drawing a Bead on Curriculum" (Norcross, Ga.: Great Commission Publications).

4.   Joe Taylor Ford, *Sourcebook of Wit and Wisdom* (Communication Resources, Inc., 1996).

5.   *Selections for the Young* (Edinburgh: Committee of the General Assembly of the Free Church of Scotland for the Publication of the Works of Scottish Reformers and Divines, n.d.), 34.

8
THE VILLAGERS AND THE VILLAGE

1.   J. I. Packer, *A Quest for Godliness: The Puritan Vision of the Christian Life* (Wheaton, Ill.: Crossway Books, 1990), 22.

2.   Ibid., 23-27.

3.   S. G. DeGraaf, *Promise and Deliverance*, vol. 1 (Ontario: Paideia Press, 1977), 20.

4.   Edward T. Welch, *When People Are Big and God Is Small* (Phillipsburg, N.J.: Presbyterian and Reformed Publishers, 1997), 157, 165, 172, 174.

5.   Ibid., 179.

6.   DeGraaf, *Promise and Deliverance*, 25.

7.   "Teacher Feature" in *Ready, Set, Teach!*, ed. Sue Jakes, Great Commission Publications (Summer 1996).

9
FOR CHRIST'S CROWN AND COVENANT

1.   *New Geneva Study Bible*, R. C. Sproul, ed. (Nashville: Thomas Nelson, 1995), note on Genesis 15:17.

2.   Ed Waldron, "Fruit That Remains," *The Southern Charity Ledger*, a publication of Palmer Home for Children, Columbus, Miss. (Spring, 1997).

3.   *Trinity Hymnal*, (Atlanta, Ga.: Great Commission Publications, Inc., 1990), 419, used by permission from Dr. Edmund P. Clowney.

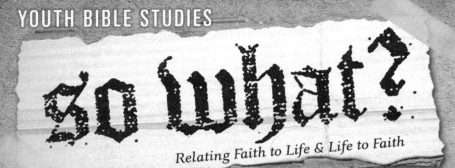

# show me Jesus™

**Teaching kids the covenant from Genesis to Revelation**

**TODDLER · PRESCHOOL · YOUNGER ELEMENTARY · MIDDLE ELEMENTARY**

# KIDS' QUEST

*Teaching Children Bible Truths*

## KIDS' QUEST! CATECHISM CLUB

## PILGRIM'S PROGRESS

www.childrenspilgrimsprogress.org

**Beginning Kids' Quest** *(ages 4–5)*
*First Catechism* Questions 1–46
(36 lessons)

**Elementary Kids' Quest** *(grades 1–6)*
*First Catechism* Questions 1–150
(36 lessons)

*Pilgrim's Progress*
*(grades 2–6)*
Children go on
an unforgettable
journey packed with
life-changing biblical
truths. (13 lessons)

**GREAT COMMISSION PUBLICATIONS**

www.gcp.org | 800-695-3387